D0374914

NASH

NASH

THE OFFICIAL BIOGRAPHY

AS TOLD TO REBECCA PALEY,
WITH PERSONAL ANNOTATIONS BY
NASH GRIER

GALLERY BOOKS

NEW YORK   LONDON   TORONTO   SYDNEY   NEW DELHI

G

Gallery Books
An Imprint of Simon & Schuster, Inc.
1230 Avenue of the Americas
New York, NY 10020

Note to readers: Certain names have been changed.

First Gallery Books hardcover edition November 2019

GALLERY BOOKS and colophon are registered trademarks of Simon & Schuster, Inc.

For information about special discounts for bulk purchases, please contact Simon & Schuster Special Sales at 1-866-506-1949 or business@ simonandschuster.com.

The Simon & Schuster Speakers Bureau can bring authors to your live event. For more information or to book an event, contact the Simon & Schuster Speakers Bureau at 1-866-248-3049 or visit our website at www.simonspeakers.com.

Interior design by Jaime Putorti

Manufactured in the United States of America

10 9 8 7 6 5 4 3 2 1

Library of Congress Cataloging-in-Publication Data

Names: Paley, Rebecca, author.
Title: Nash : the official biography / as told to Rebecca Paley, with
   personal annotations by Nash Grier.
Description: New York : Gallery Books, 2019.
Identifiers: LCCN 2019008726| ISBN 9781501137211 (hardback) | ISBN
   9781501137228 (trade paperback)
Subjects: LCSH: Grier, Nash, 1997- | Internet personalities--United
   States--Biography. | BISAC: BIOGRAPHY & AUTOBIOGRAPHY / Personal
Memoirs.
   | BIOGRAPHY & AUTOBIOGRAPHY / Entertainment & Performing Arts. |
HUMOR /
   Form / Essays.
Classification: LCC PN1992.9236.G75 P35 2019 | DDC 791.092 [B] --dc23
LC record available at https://lccn.loc.gov/2019008726

ISBN 978-1-5011-3721-1
ISBN 978-1-5011-3726-6 (ebook)

ACKNOWLEDGMENTS

To Chad, Elizabeth, Nila, and Johnnie—thank you guys for showing me what it means to love.

To Will, Hayes, Skylynn, Ellie, and my new baby brother, Hank—you're what keeps me strong. Thank you for breathing life into everyone around you.

Huge thank you to my rep, Melinda Morris Zanoni, and my entire team at both Legacy Talent and Entertainment and Apollo Sports & Entertainment Law Group! Without them this book wouldn't exist. Here's to another one in the future!

Thank you to Simon & Schuster and the incredibly talented Rebecca Paley for helping me turn this idea into a reality.

And, finally, to everyone who has ever supported me over the years in any way, big or small—thank you a million times from the bottom of my heart. Whether you know it or not, you all have played a significant role in me becoming the person I am today. The smallest gestures of kindness and love can make all the difference in the world. I wake up every day with a smile on my face, regardless of what's happening around me, and I have all of you to thank.

PREFACE

If I know one thing it's that I know nothing at all. Now I know that sounds like a stupid way to open a book, but in my opinion, it's one of the most valuable things you can understand as a person. Over time I've had trouble with silencing my ego, finding my purpose, and latching on to the little spurts of positive energy scattered throughout life as opposed to drowning in ever present negativity. I'm as open with people as I can be. Anyone who's seen my journey unfold knows what I'm talking about. I put it *all* out there on all kinds of social media platforms—from movie sets to the front row of fashion shows, and even the bathroom, I've always felt compelled to use my experiences to connect with others. And that's just online. In "real life" I'm equally accessible. If you've come out to see me at any of the meet and greets I've done, you can attest to that. I've spent countless hours meeting thousands of people from all corners of the world. All screens/likes/views/comments aside, for me life has come to be all about connecting with others. After all, human connection is what we do it for, and when I say we, I mean everyone. Literally everyone.

That's why I was psyched when I heard there was going to be a book about me. (Also kinda freaked out, if I'm honest. Biographies are usually about dead people—so that's a good sign.) It's all good. Books are amazing. I love digital technology for the speed and ease of interacting with folks you'd never meet or get to know, but books are the original way to tell stories. (Well, maybe cave pictures were, but you get what I'm saying.)

The coolest thing about them is that everyone reads the same book differently. Each person has his or her own way of imagining the words on the page. That's why when a movie is made from a much loved book, you always hear people say, "Oh, the book's way better than the movie." What they're really saying is that they liked what they imagined in their head while reading better than what they saw on the big screen, which is what the director imagined while reading the book. I totally get that. I like the pictures in my head, too.

That's why I wanted to add my own thoughts, or the stories in *my* head, to the biography that you're about to read. *All* my thoughts, crazy, sad, happy, about who I am and the life I've lived so far—where I came from, what I believe in, who my influences are, how I've been inspired by them, what I stand for, and what I hope to achieve with my failures/successes and ultimately experiences.

But you knowing me is not all I want from this book. While reading about the wild ups and downs I've experienced in my little more than two decades on this earth, I also hope *you* will imagine your own vision of success and failure, dreams and fears, peaks and valleys. I want you to layer into my stories pictures of *your* life, both as it is and as you'd like it to be.

The purpose of this book isn't just for you to read about me but to inspire and galvanize *you* into action, so that the next book I'll be reading will be yours.

NASH

CHAPTER 1

We are starting from the way beginning, like before Facebook was even invented.

Up until the age of five, Nash lived a near perfect life—if you define perfect as living in a country club community in a southern town with big skies, perfect lawns, and perfect families, just like his. The Griers were similar to many of their neighbors in the lakeside town of Davidson, North Carolina, just twenty miles or so north of Charlotte. Nash's parents, Chad and Elizabeth, were college sweethearts before they married and settled down in the idyllic town to raise their three sons.

As far as Nash, his older brother, Will, and younger brother, Hayes, were concerned, there were no worries in or around their large house, emerald green yard, thick surrounding woods, or anywhere else the boys were free to roam. Any day of the week

Nash could be found—in his favorite football jersey and a mask that shot water out of it—running around like a maniac, riding his bike, or doing tricks with his scooter on a little ramp his dad built in the driveway. Or he'd go into the woods surrounding their backyard, where he created his own adventures by climbing trees and blazing trails. Forts were very big back in the day.

Nash was lucky to have a built-in crew for fun with his family. He and his brothers, each separated by two and a half years, spent most of their time together. And most of that time was spent outside. Other than catching the occasional episode of *Barney* or, later, *Power Rangers*, they were always outdoors roughhousing and using their imaginations for made-up games. (The first electronics in their lives, other than TV and radio, didn't come until years later, when Will got a Game Boy Color with a night-light on it, so the Grier boys could play in the dark, which Nash did all the time.) One of their favorite activities was putting Hayes in the giant swing in their front yard. Will and Nash would each grab a side, run as fast as they could, seeing how high they could throw it, and then duck under the swing before it swung back. Hayes, who was only two years old at the time, screamed and laughed as he zoomed into the air. Although he could have broken his little neck, all the boys thought it was hilarious. None more so than Hayes.

Even back then, Hayes was the Tasmanian devil.
That or a wild mustang are probably the best
representations of his spirit. Whatever is at his feet

or right in front of him is all that's in his head. That's how he lives—in the immediate. He's the crazy one in our family, but ironically he's also the most sensitive and has always had a deeper and softer caring side than anyone in the family. Hayes could break his leg and not shed a tear. But show him one of those commercials where you see animals being abused—you know "for just pennies a day, you can save a . . .!"—and he'll be crying his eyes out. Animals are his weakness.

If Hayes was the little wild man of the three, then Will was the backbone. The eldest Grier boy knew exactly what he wanted to do when he was just seven years old. "I want to play football," he declared. "I want to be in the NFL." Sports in general always played a central role in his life. Basketball, baseball, you name it—he played it. Twenty-four/seven, year-round, he was playing something. But he was always most dedicated to football.

As the middle child, Nash was the typical peacekeeper. Growing up, Nash was neutral territory, the middle ground, between the opposite poles of his brothers' personalities. If he found one of them going too far (Hayes getting a little too crazy, or Will too tough), Nash stepped in to center him with a joke or subtle shift of perspective. It wasn't anything he thought about doing. It just came as naturally as Will throwing a football through a tire, or Hayes throwing himself off a ladder.

I definitely think birth order determines a lot of stuff. I always felt a special kinship to my uncle Jason, my dad's brother, who is also the middle of three brothers, like me. I relate to his sense of humor, which defuses tension, and his ability to turn a situation toward whatever direction he wants it to go.

But even an old soul like Nash had trouble finding equilibrium when his parents sat him and his brothers down to tell them that they were getting divorced. Not that Nash totally understood what his "perfect" parents were talking about when they came into the playroom to deliver the news to Will and him. Just shy of six years old, Nash was doing cartwheels and other stuff like that, while his mom and dad gave the we-still-love-you-even-if-we-don't-love-each-other speech. And Hayes? He was just a toddler and had *no idea* what was going on.

If Nash didn't get the importance of his parents' announcement that day in the playroom, it became crystal clear soon enough. That's because life was never the same again. While his parents did the best they could to maintain all the stability and love he and his brothers had enjoyed previously, divorce is never a smooth situation. Through it all, though, Will, Nash, and Hayes always knew their mom and dad had their best interests at heart—albeit in a different way.

Their mom, Elizabeth, provided the emotional support, talking to her boys all the time, about everything, making them feel special and important. She was so good at it that it seemed redundant to Nash when his school counselor, Mr. Smith, pulled him from class one day "to sit and talk." Nash didn't mind it at all. Mr. Smith was a really cool guy, and Nash loved going to his office, because he had jelly beans and computer games. Mr. Smith was also the quarterback when they played flag football at recess. He was an all-around awesome dude. But when he tried to talk to Nash about his

POST-CHURCH SUNDAY IN DAVIDSON WITH MY MOM AND BROTHERS

feelings and thoughts surrounding his parents' divorce, it seemed strange. Nash was confused because he didn't feel like he needed anything more than what his mother had already given him.

Nash's dad, on the other hand, was always the protector. After Chad and Elizabeth split up, he moved to a house on a big piece of land with pastures, a pond, and, of course, woods. There the Grier boys had mud fights and played with BB guns. But the enormous scar across Nash's forehead that he got at that house didn't come from a misfired shot or a rock hidden in a launched mud pie. No, it came from playing video games.

Despite being late adopters, Will, Hayes, and Nash were pretty serious about video games once they got started. By the time they moved into their dad's new house, they were full on into them.

If we were having trouble beating a level of Crash Bandicoot, Jak and Daxter, or whatever it was, we sat in the basement passing the sticks back and forth no matter how long it took—until we beat it.

During the incident in question, they'd been playing Crash Bandicoot, a racing game, for seven long days, and still hadn't beaten the snow level. Finally, though, Will beat it (naturally it was Will, who succeeded in every kind of competition). Hayes and Nash just went nuts. This meant they could finally move forward in the game! Screaming and running around, the brothers high-fived and chest-bumped one another. "Yeah!" Nash yelled, pumping his fist and running as fast as he could around the back of the pool table—straight into a concrete support beam.

The next thing Nash knew, he was looking at his brother's brand-new beanbag, which he had just spent four months of his allowance on—and it was soaked in blood. The blood was Nash's, pouring from a golf-ball-size hole in his head. In that moment, he had no idea what had happened. But his brothers later explained. As soon as Nash knocked himself out on the concrete block, their dad had flown down the entire four flights of stairs of this big old house. He went from the very top of their home all the way down to the basement, barely touching a single step.

Nash came to when his dad grabbed him, threw a rag on his head, ran him to the car, and whipped to the ER, where the ER doctors sewed up the gash in his head.

Thankfully the doctor stitched it nice, because later, when Hayes fell off a wall when he was three and busted his head open, his doctor did a terrible job (sorry, bro). Even more comforting, though, looking back at it was that my dad's world would completely stop if any of us were in danger.

The house where Nash busted open his head was just one of many that he and his brothers lived in after their parents split. They moved around *a lot* after the divorce, and from each place Nash has a trove of good memories.

Their mom's first place was in the actual town of Davidson, which is such a cool college town. Davidson College's beautiful campus could be straight out of a movie. While they were living there, Stephen Curry took the private liberal arts college's basketball team to the Elite Eight of the NCAA tournament, and the town went crazy. There were parades down the street and everything.

After living in the house where Nash knocked himself out, their dad moved into another one, where a new housing development was going up across the street. So right across from their yard, there was a giant construction site filled with heavy equipment, building materials, and massive machines. Basically a boy's paradise. Whenever people weren't working on the site, Will,

Nash, and Hayes ran right over to tear it up. They'd do stuff like use steel beams and cinder blocks as an obstacle course for their bikes. Or they'd hop into the cab of a Caterpillar bulldozer or the bucket of an excavator. Sometimes they'd build forts in the half-built frames of new houses. The construction workers were good people. From the boys' footprints and bicycle-tire tracks alone, they had to know a bunch of kids were goofing around in their site. But they were cool with it—so much so that they'd leave the makeshift forts up as long as they could before they had to come down for the next phase of work.

No matter where the Grier boys went there was always adventure to be had. The woods of North Carolina are thick and pretty much everywhere. As long as they were near some woods, Nash and his brothers could find the fun.

> Once while we were living beside some particularly dense woods, my dad took a chain saw and cut through the shrubbery and tangled vines to make an opening in the shape of the number one. Then a little farther down he made another opening—in the shape of the number two. And so on until Dad had created a walkway with doors in the form of different numbers. I don't know how he came up with something so cool, but it was like our own secret universe.

Will, Hayes, and Nash didn't just move around to a bunch of different houses; they also went to a lot of different schools. Cod-

MY DAD AND ME PLAYING BALL IN THE DRIVEWAY

dle Creek, Davidson Elementary, Mount Mourne—the schools they attended depended on the district where they lived. That didn't bother Nash. He's always been able to get along in different environments, with all kinds of different people. He's a classic middle child who can fit in just about anywhere.

If there was a downside to their situation postdivorce, it was shuttling between Mom and Dad. They always seemed to be on different sides of town—and the boys were in the middle.

I won't lie; that was whack.

In the first years after their divorce, the schedule (whom the boys stayed with, and when) was a source of constant tension. There was a very strict custody schedule at first. It was Dad's every Thursday and every other weekend, Mom's the rest of the time. The boys even split Christmas, leaving their mom's at

10:45 p.m. on Christmas Eve to have Christmas morning with their dad.

Getting two of everything—even Christmas—isn't all it's cracked up to be. There were definitely those bad times when the schedule seemed to take precedence over everything else, even the boys' feelings. The arguments ("That's my day." "No it's mine!") got kind of out of hand for a while. No matter how much Chad and Elizabeth fought over their sons, Nash always knew that he had a dad who loved him a lot and a mom who loved him a lot. That was way more important and lasting than who they opened gifts with on Christmas morning. It also kept Nash and his brothers grounded as they eventually got used to life in not one but two families.

JOHNNIE BUILDING A TREE HOUSE WITH
MY TERRIBLE HELP

While Nash and his brothers were living with their mom in Davidson, she started to date a new guy, and that guy ended up becoming their stepdad.

> Now, I know stepparents can get a bad rap, especially in books, but Johnnie was and continues to be one awesome dude. He's just the nicest guy ever and really loves my mom. Those are, of course, the most important things. But he also had the sweetest house on Lake Norman, which we all moved into when he got hitched to my mom.

Elizabeth's new husband, Johnnie, had a house he built himself that sat right on Lake Norman. Nash was nine years old when they moved in, and that's the house he called home until he left North Carolina.

> That was my spot. I grew up in that house and on its small beach, which opened up onto my true backyard: Lake Norman. Although it's the largest man-made lake in North Carolina, I know every inch of that lake. It's one of my favorite places on earth.

The amount of fun Nash had on the water of Lake Norman is immeasurable. There was a zip line that started in their yard and went out to the end of their dock, so that the boys could fly through the air and dive-bomb right into the water. There were also giant hamster balls so they could walk on top of the water. His mom and stepdad weren't rich, but Johnnie could build anything. And he *would* build anything to make his new family happy. Trails and forts, even boats! So after playing in the woods for a while, Nash would take a little whaler boat out to fish, visit the marina, or see one of the many friends he had who also lived on the lake.

Lake Norman didn't just entertain Nash; it was also a money-maker for him. Because there were a bunch of golf courses around the lake, the water was filled with golf balls. Golf balls are really expensive and still good after they've been submerged in water, so Nash made a little business of diving for balls and selling them back to country club members and caddies. Wearing goggles, he spent hours hunting those white balls, which were easy to spot under water. Then he'd head with his catch to any one of the courses, where there was always someone willing to buy golf balls at a cut rate.

When Nash got a little older, his first real job also revolved around the lake. It was pumping gas at the marina closest to his house. On weekends he worked there for tips alone, but the yacht owners he pumped gas for gave big, *big* tips.

While he loved his home all year-round, summers on the lake were the most glorious thing ever. Endless days of sunshine, cold clear water, and total freedom. Nash and his friends went tubing or took their boats out for adventures. They explored every nook and cranny of Lake Norman, which is how they found a secret passageway to the smaller, neighboring Lake Davidson. The two lakes, divided by the interstate, are supposed to be completely separate. But one day Nash and his buddies found an opening, about six feet high and four feet wide, with water flowing through it under the interstate. Always up for the unknown, they pulled the motor up on their small whaler boat and floated through. But upon entering the passageway, they got stuck in a spot packed full with branches, debris, hundreds of fish, and snakes. Unable to get through, they had to back the boat out and drive it back to the house, where they immediately got Nash's stepdad, Johnnie, to return to the passageway with them. (He was as game as they were.) Nash, his friends, and Johnnie wound up clearing out the entire thing, so that they could go from lake to lake without leaving the water. As far as they could figure out, nobody else knew about this passageway, which is what made it so amazing.

(Of course, now that I've spilled the beans, all of Lake Norman and Lake Davidson knows.)

Anything that could happen did happen on that lake. I can't count how many times we got stranded and someone had to tow us in. We ran out of gas, hit rocks, busted holes in the bottom of boats, and sank them. Crazy stuff. We flipped Jet Skis and lost the keys to the ignition in the bottom of the lake. Some dumb kid decided to climb above the zip line my stepdad built outside our house—and hang from it upside down. Of course, he fell. Onto a bed of rocks at the very top of the zip line. He busted his head open and had to be airlifted out of there. Yup, we saw everything on that lake.

KNEEBOARDING!

Busted heads and boats aside, Lake Norman was as close to perfection as Nash could imagine. As the years went by, he had gone to so many schools that he had friends all around the lake, which connects eight counties. They'd meet up at an island, a house, or a dock to go jet-skiing or double-tubing or just hang out. There were so many great things to do on the lake: building rope swings, snorkeling, kneeboarding, or wakeboarding.

Wakeboarding is the best. Riding the wake behind a boat on a board, it feels like you can just keep going forever. Those were the times, hanging with my friends in a squad of four or five Jet Skis or boats.

Nothing beat those summers when Nash could just walk out the back door of his house, get on the lake, and fly. Easy and free. They were so amazing—and so unlike the secret, internal pressure that was beginning to creep up on him as he entered sixth grade at his newest school.

CHAPTER 2

In sixth grade Nash started at Davidson Day School, a rigorous private school his brother Will had already attended for a few years by the time he got there. Technically, Nash should have been in seventh grade, but he was "reclassed," meaning he had to repeat the year. It wasn't because he had trouble in school, either academically or socially. Both of Nash's brothers were also reclassed. That's because they were really big into sports and wanted to have that extra year for a leg up.

Football might have been Will's passion ever since he could remember, but Nash was on the exact same path as his older brother. Just as he followed Will to Davidson Day, he followed him to combines, recruiting camps, the whole nine yards. At the age of thirteen, Nash had a highlight reel (just like Will) and played quarterback for the JV Davidson Day Patriots (Will was quarterback of the varsity team).

THE GLORY DAYS

In college and in the pros, football is a year-round sport. And that's also what it was at Davidson Day. Every year the state championships were held the last week in November—and every year, the new season of football started with its first day of practice one week after that.

Only one week off! That's insane, right?

Not only was football a year-round sport at Davidson Day, but it was pretty much seven days a week as well.

Any day of the week, if Davidson Day students looked out of a school window, they'd see a hundred people on the field practicing football. If the team wasn't out doing full-field workouts to practice their agility, footwork, and plays, then the players occupied the weight room. Every single day. That is except Friday, because Friday was game day, which was the craziest day of the week. On Fridays members of the football team wore their Davidson Day Patriots team jerseys to school, where everyone spent the day hyping them up for the game later that day. While most kids might have been goofing off or resting up on the weekend, the Davidson Day football team spent Saturday watching the tape of the previous Friday's game. Football dominated the culture of the school—and Nash's dad was the one who created the whole thing.

Chad, who played quarterback for the East Carolina Pirates for two years and later for the Spiders at the University of Richmond, started the football program at Davidson Day. The school didn't even own a football before Nash's dad came on the scene. Although he worked in the tech sector, football is Chad's passion, and as soon as he arrived at the school he poured his heart and soul into creating a top-notch team. With Chad as coach, the Davidson Day Patriots were state champions four times in five years.

The recipe to his success was no secret: work, work, and more work. Will, Nash, and Hayes's dad was hard on the whole team. Every season started with an annual camping trip to Camp Arrowhead about two hours west of Davidson. For an entire week, surrounded by the picturesque setting of pine, oak, and hickory along the shores of a beautiful—albeit small—lake, Chad and his team got serious. Working out, eating, and training were the only three things they did from the moment they woke up at 6 a.m. to the minute they went to bed at 9 p.m. Nash felt like he'd hardly fallen asleep when it was already the next day and time to repeat the whole thing all over again. The trip was all three-a-days: one workout in the morning, a little break, one workout in the middle of the day, a little break, then one workout in the evening.

If you've never heard of "three-a-days," even if you've played football or are a fan, that's because most teams do two-a-days. Not three-a-days! When we went to Lake Arrowhead, by the third workout you were so tired it felt like you were floating. And we did that for a week! The tradition my dad began as soon as he started the football program was that if you made it back alive from that camp, then you made it on the team.

Their dad was equally hard on the team off the field. He maintained a strict attitude toward everyone's grades. There was a certain GPA a student had to have to play football at Davidson Day, but he created even higher benchmarks and goals for his players to reach. That was important because half the people on the team were brand-new to the school, and not typical Davidson students.

Chad loved football, but his main drive was "How do I use the game to change people's lives?" To that end, he would go to schools with underserved students and just talk to people—kids, parents, and educators looking for something better for the students with promise. He took so many guys out of the worst situations and got them full scholarships to this fancy, private, K–12 school, where ninth graders were taking advanced placement classes.

He wouldn't just find these kids a place at Davidson Day; he also gave many of them a place in his home. Some of the team members lived at his house for months, even years, either because these guys came from too far away or they didn't have a stable home that would support the new pressures they faced in a prep-school environment. The biggest issue was that a lot of the students on the football team had bad grades when Nash's dad started the program. Eventually, though, the football team's overall GPA was higher than that of any of the other teams at the school. Again, it was Chad who did that. There are so many kids in college right now who would have not been anywhere if it weren't for him. Austin is just one example of many. When he started at Davidson Day, Austin wasn't a great student and not much better at football. He also had to live with Chad and the Grier boys, because he was from the Beatties Ford Road area. At the time, it was officially ranked the number-one neighborhood in Charlotte for violent crime. Why Chad had pushed to get a full scholarship for Austin was totally unclear. He saw something in Austin nobody else could, and he turned out to be right.

Over the next four years at the school, Nash watched Austin turn into a completely different person. From one year to the next, the changes in him were radical. From a physical standpoint, he went from a kid who subsisted on junk food to a healthy athlete who treated his body like a temple by exercising religiously and eating nutritious meals. He threw himself into every practice and game to become one of Davidson Day's top players. But Austin didn't just change physically. He also radically transformed his mindset. Whereas he started ninth grade shy and insecure, he graduated a confident leader. Austin, whose brothers followed him to Davidson Day, earned a full scholarship to West Point.

You'd be surprised how much you can do if you just try.

How Chad changed Austin's life so completely and permanently made a huge impression on Nash. He appreciated the fact that his dad was so good at using football as a vehicle for evolution of the whole person, because Chad didn't just preach the physicality of the sport. He talked just as much about how football is a mental game. Of course part of that included getting inside your opponent's head. But not by trash-talking; Nash's dad would never stand for that. No, he insisted his players be good and smart sportsmen. He taught his players to use subtle body language and other techniques to gain the advantage.

His father's more important mental takeaway revolved around the nature of the game itself. Each play in football is only about six to eight seconds long. Then it's a dead ball. Then back to playing another six to eight seconds. Stop. Dead ball. Play. Repeat. It's natural to use the breaks within play to zone out and just catch your breath. But Chad taught his team that during the time in between plays they should be thinking: assessing the situation that just occurred and strategizing what should happen next. This kind of mental prep allowed them to eliminate all the extra calculations and decision making during the game, so that all they had to concentrate on was their performance, which is the biggest determinant to the outcome of the game.

The lesson that went far beyond football, for Nash, is that there really is no such thing as downtime. And there was no one Chad drove that lesson home harder with than his three sons.

His rule was "Because you're my kid, I have to go ten times harder on you." He said this to Will, Nash, and Hayes all the time, and it was true for a couple of different reasons. The first was to negate any appearance of special treatment. Every member of a team has to be treated equally.

You just can't have that. I'd been on a team before where a dad coach favored his kid, and it always turns out bad.

Then there was the not so insignificant fact that Will and Nash received a lot of financial aid because of football. Davidson Day cost more than $17,000 a year! There was no way the Grier family could afford that. Just like Austin and many other kids on the team, Nash got an opportunity for a world-class education because of football—and the fact that his dad was the coach. So yeah, he had to be on the top of his game.

That meant a lot of practice *outside* of their regular grueling schedule with the team. From circle tosses to one-knee drills and sprint outs, Nash's dad lived up to his promise to go hard on him and his brothers. He had them practice their footwork for hours and hours in the backyard, so much so that they dug out paths of dirt in the lawn.

If you went back to our old house, you'd probably still find the grooves of the first step, second step, third step, and plants of our three-step drops.

Just like those markings in the grass, a three-step drop is imbedded in Nash, because he spent so much time mastering it. The relentless quest for perfection by breaking down each element of an act and then practicing it over and over and over again until it's pure muscle memory resulted in an amazing kind of freedom. When Nash was in a game, the adrenaline pumping, and had to do a three-step drop, he didn't even need to think about it. He just did it.

That lesson of hard work freeing you up for greater creations, like so many other lessons my dad taught me, extends way past the world of football, where I first learned it. My dad understood that a lot of aspects of the game go hand in hand with life. Teamwork. Sacrifice. Diligence. All of these and more were characteristics that you develop on the field, but can help you with the rest of your life.

That was in the forefront of Chad's mind when he pushed football in his family, which Will was more than happy to pursue. A freak athlete, Will could have played any sport he wanted to. He was just that insanely physically talented. As a five-year-old playing

NASH'S FIRST MIDDLE SCHOOL
FOOTBALL GAME

on a soccer team, coaches of opposing teams asked to take Will out of the game because he was making too many goals! (Chad didn't keep his son from playing but instead taught him to pass the ball. So little Will would run with the ball and wait in front of the goal for a teammate to catch up, then he'd pass to him and that kid would score.) Other than football, Will loved to play basketball, which he was equally amazing at. When Will was just three years old, his dad taught him to shoot a basketball on a ten-foot rim. By the time he was in sixth grade, Will could dunk a basketball! Nash would travel around the entire country watching him play future members of the NBA, of which he could have easily been one.

But Will loved football the most and dedicated his heart and soul to it, so that by the time he was in high school, he was a legend in their part of the country. As the quarterback of a team that only lost twice in five years, Will broke a national record when he threw 837 yards in a single game. He was the Gatorade Player of the Year, National Player of the Year, Mr. Football USA, and on and on. Dubbed the best player in the nation, he got offers from a slew of Division I colleges before he committed to play quarterback at the University of Florida.

While he was at Davidson Day, Will ran the school. Everyone looked up to Nash's big brother. And it wasn't just Davidson Day students who were obsessed with and idolized him. People came from all over the region to see the myth in action. His games would be huge! There were crowds everywhere, spilling over from the stands and out onto the hills. That was the impact he had.

Meanwhile, Nash was supposed to be next in line to fill Will's shoes!

I was always Will Grier's brother.

He was a quarterback just like his brother and, according to his dad, had the same potential. When Nash entered seventh grade, he first began to contemplate the idea of succeeding his brother, the star athlete to end all high school star athletes. It was around this time that he asked his dad while they were driving to school, "How do I match up to Will when he was my age?"

Maybe Chad sensed his middle son's doubt, but his answer was decisive and totally surprising to Nash: "You are ten times better than Will was."

That was mind-blowing, mainly because I didn't think you could be better than Will.

Will, who was also in the car, agreed with their dad. It wasn't a comment on Nash's physical prowess. There was no question Will was the better athlete. Nash's skills were a result of Will's incredible football career. Watching and trying to emulate him, Nash developed earlier and at a quicker rate, which is common for younger siblings.

Nash appreciated his dad and Will's vote of confidence, but he was still deeply unsure about the whole thing.

Why was he following in his brother's footsteps? Did he want to be in this position in the first place?

The more he thought about his situation, the more Nash began to question what it was that he really wanted. While he did love football, he wasn't sure there wasn't something else out there that he'd love more. Nash definitely knew he didn't need or want to play the game as much as Will did.

Everyone is so different, and yet Nash was doing the exact same thing as his older brother simply because he didn't have the time or opportunity to experience anything else. That didn't seem like a good reason to decide what he was going to do with his life—or at least the next eight years of it. Could it be possible that Nash actually belonged somewhere else, that maybe football wasn't really for *him*?

This might not seem like a big deal, but in the Grier family, the idea that he would veer one step from the football field was a really big deal. So almost as soon as these thoughts took hold in his mind, he knew he had to talk to his mom about them.

My mom is the ultimate wisdom. She says that my brothers and I are like her three souls. She feels a connection with each one of us that is very different but equally strong. Because she brought us into the world, she feels it's her purpose in life to help us in any way we can. Her love is truly unconditional. That's why I feel like there's nothing I can't tell my mom. Every kid needs someone who is always on their side, whether it's a teacher, counselor, or coach. But I know how lucky I am that that person also happens to be my mom.

Elizabeth, Nash's mom, was characteristically supportive from day one.

I CAN'T TELL IF THAT'S MY MOM OR MY MOM'S TWIN SISTER

"What do you think?" Nash asked her after spilling all the stuff he had been mulling over.

"Do whatever your heart says," she said. "It's your life."

My life?

That was the first time Nash really had the thought that this was actually his life. It had never occurred to him consciously that he could create an existence of his very own. If he hadn't heard that message from his mom, Nash might never have strayed from the path he was on and found his way onto the one he's on now.

> *It was in this moment that I thought, <u>All right.</u>*
> *<u>It is my life. I guess I can do whatever I want.</u>*
> *<u>I'm pretty</u> sure.*

Nash didn't decide to quit football over one conversation. It was more like fifty. He went through a painful couple of months, going back and forth, talking to his mom, weighing the pros and cons, and finally deciding.

Once Nash had made up my mind that he didn't want to do football anymore, he had another problem on his hands: How was he going to tell his dad?

It took a while for him to get up the courage, but finally one day when they were in the car, Nash turned to his dad from the passenger seat.

> *I was so scared that I don't even know what I said, but I got my point across somehow.*

"Wait," Nash's dad said. "Are you saying you're just going to throw all that hard work away?"

"Yeah, I guess. Maybe I'm just going to throw it all away."

Father and son got into a heated conversation, because Chad thought Nash was crazy as hell. And maybe at the time it seemed like he was, but there was just something inside him telling him what he had to do.

It doesn't hurt to be open-minded.

"I'm done," Nash told his dad. "I'm *quitting*."

Nash's dad wasn't the only one who didn't understand. Going to school after the news got out that he was quitting football was totally weird. Nash's teammates weren't mad or anything negative. Just seriously confused. "What happened, bro?" they all asked. Nash didn't have an answer for them, at least not a good one. So things were awkward for a while. Nash had had such a specific role before as quarterback of the middle school team, where eighty kids depended on him for pretty much every single snap of the game. Now he didn't know what his role was.

I was floating, through the end of the football season and right into springtime, when I found myself without anything to do, which I did not like. I still loved sports, and it felt like all I knew how to do.

In need of something to replace football, Nash found lacrosse. That spring was only the second year Davidson Day had a team. But

Nash, who had always watched the sport because of friends who played it at other schools, admired it. So he decided to give it a try.

Nash might have quit football, but he still was very much under the influence of his father, who taught him the value of hard work. As he launched into this new sport, he spent hours in front of the computer, reading about lacrosse's history, watching videos of important plays, and researching its fundamentals. Then he went out and did it. Beyond practicing with the team, he spent extra hours every day throwing balls against the wall, working on his technique and his muscle memory just as his dad had done with Will and him in their backyard.

All the skill in the world won't keep you from getting outworked.

Nash fell in love with lacrosse. He was obsessed with the sport, which seemed to combine the elements of so many other sports. It had the high contact of hockey, the fast pace and nonstop defensive and offensive play of soccer, and the throwing of baseball. But lacrosse also felt special to him, because it was his own thing. No one else in the Grier family knew the first thing about it, and Nash kind of liked that.

I wanted to have something where I was the one determining my fate.

As it turned out, he did a pretty good job. Nash ended up making the varsity lacrosse team as a seventh grader, his first year playing the game!

No matter what you're doing, do it to the best of your abilities. Whether you're flying a plane or washing dishes, focus on doing everything the absolute best you can and watch how fulfilling life becomes.

The difference in playing lacrosse rather than football was instant for Nash. Before he quit the football team, he loved to play games but dreaded practice. Meanwhile he had to spend more than half his life on that field, practicing. Nash *hated* that feeling. With lacrosse, however, he was always psyched to get on the field. If they had a game, he would be itching all day to get out there, looking out the window, almost unable to wait until it was time to go.

I remember thinking it was insane that I could like something so much.

While researching lacrosse on the internet, Nash learned it is America's oldest sport. It was here before baseball, before any Pilgrims were even here. Having started as a game played by Native Americans, lacrosse is America's original pastime. There are some tribes who still continue to practice and play lacrosse today.

When Nash's team at Davidson Day went to the nationals in lacrosse, they ended up playing Six Nations, a team of Iroquois from New York State. The way these guys played was completely mind-opening to Nash. Generally the sport is played with sticks that have aluminum shafts, but the Six Nations team played with more traditional wooden sticks, which are heavier and therefore harder to move around and shoot. They were so graceful, though; they made those sticks look like they were lighter than air. Nash saw something in the Six Nations that day that never left him.

Flowing as a perfect team, they were all on the same course. They all knew what their goal was and how to go after it. As an athlete, Nash was always good when it came to the mental game. He'd create things in his mind that overcame whatever he might have lacked in physical ability. Strategy is the secret to winning. But Nash, who had nothing on the Six Nations, was deeply inspired by their example.

Whatever you want to do—paint, make music, or play lacrosse—you have to know what your goal is and how to achieve it. Once you have that all set out, the rest is just flow and artistry.

NASH'S

SUGGESTED READING LIST

(in no particular order)

- *His Dark Materials* by Philip Pullman

- *Lyra's Oxford* by Philip Pullman

- *The Four Agreements: A Practical Guide to Personal Freedom* by Don Miguel Ruiz

- *Tangerine* by Edward Bloor

- *Frindle* by Andrew Clements

CHAPTER 3

The summer before his sophomore year, Nash was lying on his bed one night checking out his Facebook feed. Three friend requests had come in over the last hour, and Nash accepted. With well past two thousand friends, he sometimes found it hard to keep up.

Two thousand friends was a lot for an average kid like him at the time, and they seemed to have come overnight. Two hundred quickly went to four hundred and, before he knew it, a thousand—way more friends than anyone else he knew. It made sense, though. Having attended five schools before landing at Davidson Day and moving to almost as many neighborhoods, he had made a lot of real-life friends from different places all around Charlotte. Nash also always connected his friends, spread across five counties and all around Lake Norman, so that they became a kind of network of their own.

I guess it was just like how a lot of other things are magnified on the internet; my friends on social media grew exponentially out of my real life.

While Nash was checking out Facebook that night, his dad's voice entered his head. It was just a few weeks before the new school year was set to start, and Nash had a lot better things to do than be on the internet. Although it had been three years since he quit playing football, Nash continued to live almost every day the life lessons he got from his dad's coaching. When he had been on the team, Chad had a bunch of quotes that he liked to use, which sometimes seemed corny or confusing in the moment but always hit Nash later. Well, the one that hit Nash in that particular moment thinking about the challenges ahead of him that year in school was "Hard work works."

It was nice interacting with kids on Facebook, seeing what cool stuff they were up to, getting inspired by it, and in turn reaching back out to them with my particular jam. But right now, I told myself, I needed to focus on other, more important things—namely, school and lacrosse.

Nash knew the coming academic year was the time when there would be an explosion of recruitment action for college. Just like with soccer, lacrosse recruiting typically happens a lot earlier in high school than other sports like football or baseball.

(Actually a lot of soccer recruiting occurs even earlier than high school, which is madness.)

If you are going to play Division I lacrosse in college, you will be fully committed to a school by the end of your sophomore year. That was 110 percent Nash's plan, which meant he didn't have time for Facebook or anything else. So in a show of true commitment, that night he deleted each and every one of his social media accounts.

With an easy click of a button it was gone, all of it. But that was just the start. Then began the real hard work. Nash had already come pretty far as a lacrosse player, but now he was laser-focused. As a sophomore, he was starting on Davidson Day's varsity team as a second-line midfielder, or middie. The team had matured. Not only had the original team members improved with time, but their early success attracted good athletes from other sports at the school, growing the squad into one that competed in the highest-level tournaments in the country.

And that was just the Davidson Day team. Nash played for a slew of other teams, including a traveling team and a national team. He played all over the place, getting as much lacrosse in as he could. Like the Six Nations team members, Nash had a clear goal in mind. Still, he had to strategize correctly to get there. His goal was to get on track for an Ivy League college, and although he was taking a lot of AP science courses, lacrosse was the only way he was going to get there. His ticket to a great college was his chosen sport. That was fine with him, because he continued to be as obsessed with lacrosse as when he had first started. There was not a moment during that period of his life that he didn't have a lacrosse stick in his hand.

I even slept with it!

Every waking moment (and maybe some sleeping ones as well) was devoted to lacrosse. Nash arrived at school each day at 8 a.m. with a bag full of lacrosse balls, another bag filled with water bottles, and about five bucks for Subway or some other cheap lunch. After opening the fence to school and letting himself in, he would begin working out before classes started. As soon as he was officially done with classes for the day Nash was right back out on the field, doing drills and shooting for hours on end. Davidson Day had a huge wall with a net on either side of the field, which was a godsend for Nash, since it kept him from losing any balls (lacrosse balls, rubber with a concrete center, are very expensive and very easy to lose).

That was the best feeling, getting out on that field with a stick and ball and a clear goal to strive for. So I usually stayed at school until 8 p.m., long after the sun had gone down.

It was during the spring of 2013, during his sophomore year and the height of the lacrosse season, when Nash got sucked back into social media. Vine, the site where users could share six-second looping videos, had just been launched by Twitter the previous January and it was *the . . . new . . . thing . . .* at school. Everyone was hooked on these quick-hit videos that could be anything from a girl twerking behind a TV newscaster giving a live report on air to a mash-up of Whitney Houston's "I Will Always Love You" and a shrieking goat. Anything and everything that could be captured and resonate with viewers within six seconds was fair game.

Although Nash didn't have an account himself, he was always checking out these cool little videos at school on everyone else's phones. But when he wanted to show a friend who lived on Lake Norman a crazy Vine of a dude dropkicking someone else in the back, he decided to sign up. It started innocently enough. No big deal, right? But he wasn't back on social media more than a week when he began to think, *I want to make people laugh like this.*

Nash was never a performer in the sense of doing school plays or anything like that, but he always loved to get a rise out of his friends and classmates. Making stupid faces, busting on his brother Will's terrible accent in a Spanish class they had together, or pretending to fall when he handed in a test to a teacher: that was all part of a typical school day in the life of Nash Grier.

Nash never participated in chorus or theater, but he had been taking Davidson Day's improv class ever since arriving at the school in sixth grade.

The teacher, Ms. Gertie, was awesome. Every class she came up with some exercise to fuel our imaginations and challenge our willingness to make fools of ourselves. One of my favorites was when she put two chairs together and said, "This is a park bench." Then she chose two people to sit down and act out whatever came into their minds. If you messed up by breaking whatever scene was being created, you had to get off the bench. One by one, everyone in the class got a chance to sit on the bench, because whenever people laughed, got nervous, or just couldn't think of anything to do, Ms. Gertie told them to stand up. Well, once I got on that bench I stayed there forever. I would be on that bench for the entire class cooking up stuff. I got a high coming up with funny stuff that got the whole class laughing.

Nash always got an A in improv. How Ms. Gertie graded her students was pretty funny in itself. There was a period every day right before lunch when the entire upper school would file into the auditorium for various announcements, which lasted about a half hour. Each semester one of those daily sessions was devoted strictly to Nash's improv class, when he and the other kids in the class would have to do one of their exercises in front of the whole school. As if that weren't a tough enough assignment, how the rest of the school responded to their performances formed the basis of their grades. So if someone killed it, that was an A. (A lot of kids who took the class thinking it was going to be an easy A ended up hurting their GPA with improv. If they weren't prepared to bust out some crazy energy, it was reflected in their grade.)

Nash's first Vines were basically mini improv sessions, physical comedy like messing around with teachers or jokes such as "how guys fart versus how girls fart." He did whatever a normal teenage kid would do with six seconds of video that he could shoot out to all his friends at school to watch that same day. One early rule of thumb: the dumber Hayes—who was then thirteen—and Nash looked, the better.

Case in point: a classic Grier Vine from back in the day.

A tight shot of Nash jet-skiing, but when the camera pulls away, the viewer sees him riding a Jet Ski on top of a trailer.

I know. Cool.

It might not have been high art, but kids Nash knew laughed and shared it among themselves, which was all he was really looking for anyway.

Nash never posted any videos with the intent of getting an audience greater than the people at school. While he was getting a lot of props at Davidson Day for his Vines, he never could have dreamed up what happened next.

It all started with a Vine he posted that July with Skylynn, his half sister. (Nash was almost twelve years old when she was born to Johnnie and Elizabeth.) Nash's little sister, four years old at the time he started doing stuff with Vine, was one of his favorite

MY FIRST PHOTO SHOOT WITH SKYLYNN (WHICH WE DID OURSELVES AT HOME)

subjects. Pretty much anything she did, from dancing to commenting on a music video, was good for a laugh. The setup for this particular video was Nash asking Skylynn, "What's wrong with America today?"

In her tiny cute voice, she answered definitively, "They. Need. Jesus."

People who followed Nash on Vine liked it, but no more so than anything else he posted. At least not that he could tell. But somehow, the Vine made its way to the attention of Tiffany Semashko, who had 300,000 followers on the social media site at the time. That was a heck of a lot of followers, especially considering she was just a normal high school student in Arkansas. When Tiffany re-Vined the video, Nash got 10,000 followers overnight.

That wasn't the end of crazy. A week and twenty new Vines later, Nash had 50,000 followers. This thing began to take on a life of its own. While he kept doing what he had been doing from the start—just goofing around—more and more people were taking notice. In July, Nash topped 200,000 followers! In less than three weeks, Nash went from 2,000 followers to a hundred times that. Little did he know that was only the tip of the iceberg. At this point, Nash began gaining about 100,000 new followers a week on the video-sharing site, where since April he had posted about 124 Vines.

It's one thing to watch numbers on a computer screen increase, but it's a totally different experience getting recognized on the street by strangers.

The first time someone came up to Nash and asked for a picture, he was in the SouthPark Mall in Charlotte. A girl approached him, clearly very excited. He couldn't imagine why.

"Can I have a picture?" she said.

"Yeah," he said, more confused than anything else.

After she took a photo of the two of them together, Nash turned to the friends he was with for confirmation that he hadn't just hallucinated the whole incident.

"Yo, did you guys see that?" he asked. "What just happened?"

They shrugged their shoulders, just as mystified as Nash. His friends definitely didn't know what was so special about him. Quickly, though, the phenomenon of people asking for Nash's picture became a very real and regular thing. At the mall, in a restaurant with his family after church, on the beach, mostly girls wanted a photo with him. When his car was at a stoplight, a lot of times people in the car next to his would be waving at him like crazy. He was naturally weirded out, but for the most part Nash could handle the new attention. It got out of control, however, at one of Will's football games, when forty fans for the opposing team crossed over to Davidson Day's side of the field to get pictures—of Nash! Bombarded by so many people at once, he just started laughing. Basically, he didn't know what else to do.

If you see any of the photos from that day, I look insane.

By the time Nash returned to school in the fall of 2013, he had 1.4 million followers on Vine! To put that in perspective, at the time, having one million followers on the site was unusual for anyone, including celebrities. So the fact that Nash, a high school junior in North Carolina, had more than that was mind-boggling.

He had more followers—*way* more followers—than Miley Cyrus or Justin Bieber. *What?* The only celebrity ahead of him (or at least a celebrity that Nash had ever heard of before) was Harry Styles from the band One Direction. In addition to their sheer numbers, his followers came from all over world. They weren't just American girls but people from as far away as Australia and Saudi Arabia.

Everything happening was exciting but also deeply confusing. The truth is Nash wasn't sure *what* was happening.

This was in the early days of social media, which was evolving as rapidly as Nash's profile. Snapchat didn't really exist in the way it does now. Being a social media presence wasn't yet a thing. There were YouTubers, but that was it in terms of any kind of career or fame via social media. And even that wasn't so big.

Nash was becoming famous—sort of. But for what? Trying to make his friends laugh at school? That didn't make sense, at least not in the world as Nash knew it. It was one thing to be recognized because you were an actor or musician or model. But back then, to be a normal person getting the reaction of a celebrity was bizarre.

It wasn't only strangers out in public who started treating Nash differently. The kids at school gave off a whole new vibe. At Davidson Day, cameras were always on Nash. Because he had gotten his start on Vine by joking around, some of the other students got the crazy idea that "if we can get a video of this clown, maybe we can get something out of it, too."

To be honest, I don't know what they were
thinking. All I know is that once my videos starting

going viral, everyone at that school pissed me off. Well, not everyone—but mostly. The only people I could hang out with, other than my family, were my AP biology teacher, Ms. Brown, who was my champion, and the guys on the lacrosse team.

Nash was still very much on his original path of playing lacrosse to get into college. But with his newfound online fame, it got a whole lot harder to do.

By that point, Nash had probably played more than a hundred lacrosse tournaments. It didn't matter if they involved seven teams, twenty, or a hundred. They were all highly competitive events. In general, lacrosse is a very aggressive sport where the talk can be just as belligerent as the play. That's part of the culture of the game. But it isn't just the players who engage in trash-talk. Parents, siblings, fans of the team—anyone watching will yell stuff. As a player, you can hear *and* feel the tension coming from the stands. That's just part of the game!

Once people started recognizing Nash, the level of aggression aimed at him (and consequently his team) grew exponentially. "Look! That's Nash Grier on that team," he could hear people saying. And if he couldn't hear them, he could see them pointing at him. Meanwhile, players from other teams in the tournament showed up to watch games Nash's team was playing, which wasn't the norm. Nash didn't like being singled out because of his videos while he was on the lacrosse field. This wasn't the kind of attention he was looking for.

That's exactly what happened as soon as Nash's team arrived on the turf fields of Mazeppa Road Park, near Charlotte, for a tournament. As soon as he got there, he started to hear insults from the stands.

"There's the funny guy."

"Pretty boy."

"Hey, big star!"

He hated it but just kept his eyes forward, pretending like he couldn't hear anything, even though everyone knew better.

On the field, the energy directed toward Nash by the members of the opposing team was different but no less hurtful. The game of lacrosse can get so dirty. Although there are lots of strict regulations—like the butt of your stick can't be coming out of the rubber at the bottom, or the mesh pocket of the head can't be too deep—players find ways to mess with one another. They jab each other in the side with their metal shaft when no one is looking or send an attack while a player is waiting for the ball.

Ultimately, lacrosse is a contact sport. So when players want to show you what's up, they do it with their bodies. You can go a whole game without saying a word, but say so much with your stick.

That day at Mazeppa Park, Nash could feel the people on the field singling him out. Whenever he took off his helmet, he would have a bunch of people staring at him with a look that said "I need to deck you really hard and right now."

As the game went on, the aggression toward him continued to escalate until it seemed like Nash was more important than even the ball itself.

Usually, ground balls in lacrosse are very, very significant. When the ball's not in the air, or in someone's stick, but on the ground—meaning it's in no one's possession—whoever picks it up gains possession of the ball for their team. Lacrosse players are taught that there is nothing more important than getting that ground ball. They can't live without that ball. Without it, they are on defense and can't do anything but try to get that ball back.

While Nash was playing in the tournament, he started to see members of the other team peel off when a pack was going for a ground ball and head for him instead! If anyone got close enough, they'd check him right in the shoulders.

They might have been coming for Nash, but Nash was still going for the ball. At one point near the end of the game, he picked up a ground ball and ran for midfield. Everyone was getting in formation for a fast break as they carried up to the attack. Someone on tackle came off to play Nash quickly. Meanwhile, another member of the opposing team was coming at Nash from the other side. With both coming at him at top speed, he dodged the one on the left only to find himself face-to-face with the other one. Nash was trying to split him, but he also needed to protect the ball. He couldn't run with it against his chest (that's illegal), so Nash decided to do a swim move. That's where you hold the stick carrying the ball over the defender's head while you dodge him.

This might not have been the smartest decision, because the player who was after him (in fact, he had been after Nash the whole game) was six foot four and huge. Nash went for it anyway. But as Nash was coming down on the swim, the player from the opposing team got under him to hit him way below the shoulders, deep and hard in his flank. It was the nastiest hit Nash had ever felt.

If you ever held a lacrosse stick, they seem very light. But they hurt! I have scars all over my body from those things, because, while there are penalties for hitting too high (like around the head), shoulders and below are pretty much okay.

The hit wasn't actually the worst part. It was what happened right *after* the hit. The force of the strike against Nash's side from his opponent was so strong that it sent him flying backward

(but just gotta add, I still had the ball).

The hit, the speed Nash had been moving at, his full weight, and gravity all collided as Nash's head hit the hard turf. All that energy was thrown right into his skull.

When you get a concussion, you feel your brain shaking, which is what happened to me. The last thing I remembered was seeing my helmet snap up and back as my back hit the ground. Then I blacked out.

CHAPTER 4

Nash was so mad. Guys had been gunning for him on the lacrosse field ever since he'd gotten some notoriety on social media, but the tournament at Mazeppa Park was the first time he ever got a concussion from it. And now, because of the blow his head took, he couldn't practice or play in any games for at least six weeks!

Those were the doctor's orders. Nash couldn't even do certain schoolwork; weird stuff. As much as he wanted to be back on the field of play, Nash wasn't going to mess with his brain any more than he already had. So he had a break in which he was forced to sit around and just think.

Nash lived in two different worlds. There was Nash the Davidson Day junior who went to school every day, played lacrosse, and hoped one day to make it to an Ivy League school. Then there was the Nash whose online presence was growing exponentially by the day. He wasn't sure where either Nash was headed, but one thing was totally clear: his two worlds weren't only interfering with each other. They had collided.

During his agonizing six-week ban from lacrosse, Nash dove even deeper into social media and continued to pick up followers. But it wasn't just online peers who were noticing what he was up to. Businesses had taken notice, too.

It makes sense that companies and brands would approach someone like Nash, who reached so many kids. With a quick tweet or Facebook post, he could have as much impact, or more, than those paid ads that pop up all over web pages and which nobody ever looks at. But at the time he got his first offer, he didn't know any of that. It was from a phone-case company, which reached out to him to say they'd pay him a couple of hundred bucks to post about their product. As with the girl who approached Nash in the mall for a photo that first time, he couldn't believe they were for real. Nash could make the same amount of money as mowing four lawns—in two minutes posting about a phone case? They didn't have to ask twice. His answer was "Hell, yes!"

If Nash couldn't believe the deal from the phone-case folks, he had lots of opportunities to become a believer. The phone deal was just the first of many offers that started to come in from businesses as far away as London and Israel. Nash started to get several emails or phone calls *every day* from people wanting to know if they could manage him, hire him to post about their product, show up to their event, or license his videos.

Part of me wanted to DM them back and say "Do you know I'm just some random teenage dude in North Carolina who doesn't even have a driver's license yet?" And I might have, if there had been enough time to think about it.

As Nash's dad, who was also trying to wrap his mind around the situation, fielded calls from production companies, ad agencies, publishers, and new websites, Nash received an offer that really stood out. It was for something called MagCon—which is short for a meet-and-greet convention.

The first event of its kind, it was going to be a group of kids with big social media presences just like Nash, literally meeting and greeting their fans in real life. The inspiration for MagCon

CAMERON AND ME

came when Aaron Carpenter, a web video star from Louisiana, put on Twitter, where he had 200,000 followers, that if anyone wanted to meet him in person, he was going to be at a Dallas mall. The result was two hundred screaming girls who showed up to get a minute with him in the flesh.

Well, there were a whole lot more than two hundred fans at the first MagCon, held in Dallas in November 2013. The convention organizers had brought together about a dozen guys, a lot of whom Nash had already connected with online. There was Shawn Mendes, a Canadian musician who played acoustic guitar on a YouTube channel he started back in 2011. Aaron Carpenter was there too, as well as Jack & Jack, Jc Caylen, Taylor Caniff, Matthew Espinosa, and Carter Reynolds. Probably the most popular in the group was Cameron Dallas, who like Nash had made a name for himself by playing pranks and making fun of himself on Vine. He and Nash made an instant connection. But Nash had to give major props to the only girl at the event, Mahogany Lox, a supertalented singer, actor, and DJ whose grandfather happens to be Berry Gordy, the founder of Motown Records.

Whatever their talent or appeal, it was enough to fill up an entire hotel. The whole Sheraton in Dallas was booked out! Fans, each of whom had purchased a general admission ticket to the event and some of whom had shelled out even more for VIP passes, filled every single ballroom in the place.

Nash didn't know what to expect, but he definitely didn't expect to spend the next twelve hours meeting two-thousand-plus people!

EN ROUTE WITH JACK & JACK

MagCon was a life-changing, mind-altering, heart-exploding experience. And that description doesn't come close to doing it justice.

In a crowded ballroom, one by one, people came up to Nash to take pictures, give him a hug, say how much they cared about him, or do whatever they wanted for however long they wanted.

"Hey, Nash, I love you!"

"You saved my life."

"You changed my life."

"I use your videos to get me out of dark places."

"I get happiness from your videos."

Each and every encounter felt significant and inspirational. Having people say things no one other than his family would ever say, like "I love you," and things no one had ever said to him, like "You saved my life," was intense. Why? Nash was just a fifteen-year-old kid who had made a bunch of very short videos with the intention of making students in his high school laugh. But he found out that his efforts had a profound effect on so many people he had never met. Until now.

In that space, with all those different people, Nash went into a whole other state. A good state. Actually, a great one. Sure, part of it was exhaustion: try meeting more than two thousand people with only a short break and you might start to float as well. But there was another element at work. A sense of purpose was just beginning to come to the surface. Although he didn't recognize it as that yet, Nash knew MagCon had been an incredibly rewarding experience.

Nash definitely didn't do it for the paycheck, which turned out to be $250—the same amount he made for his first paid post about the phone case. The organizers said that's what was left for each participant after costs, etc. But Nash didn't have a problem with that. Heck, he would have been willing to do it for free at that point, since he had no idea what was involved.

I got so sick the day after MagCon, I thought I was going to die. I never get sick and never that bad, but after all the people I'd kissed and hugged, it's amazing I didn't die.

Nash returned from Dallas with a completely new perspective. Not only had meeting all those amazing people been a mind-blowing experience, but it was also pretty rad to get to skip school, fly to another city, get his own hotel room, and order whatever he wanted from room service. His family was nowhere near poor, at least not compared with most people in this world. Still, Nash wasn't accustomed to this level of luxury.

As far as I was concerned, fries delivered to my room whenever I wanted was the life.

When Nash got home from MagCon he was so energized by the experience that he made a big push to do ongoing collaborations with other social media stars just like him. The idea of social media collaboration was to take someone else's audience and Nash's audience, throw them at each other, then wait to see if there was any cross-pollination. Meaning, would some of Nash's followers land over with the other guy, and would some of his land over by Nash? Did people have the appetite to follow both channels?

That's what he did early in the game, because from what he noticed on YouTube, collaboration was the key to getting more activation and more eyeballs. He had watched hours and hours of social media personalities, like Jack and Finn Harries, a pair of British YouTubers, and Devinsupertramp, an adventure YouTuber. Nash didn't discriminate based on content or style. It was all about the audience. If he found someone who had four million views, Nash got curious about what they were doing to be so successful. Then if he liked what they did, he wanted to collaborate with them.

After watching all these YouTubers, he began reaching out to them. "Hey, do you guys have any advice for someone who's getting started?" Or, "Hey, do you guys maybe want to collab in the future? I've got this many followers."

Nash started meeting up with random old people. Well, not *old*. But old to him. At fifteen, he began hanging with guys like Alex James, who was twenty-four and at the time had a couple of million followers. Alex lived about three hours away from Nash in North Carolina, but a few times he drove all the way to pick Nash up from school so they could make videos in his car.

(Yes, I know how that sounds.)

They made about ten videos playing characters in wigs and stuff, which went viral. Beyond just the increase to Nash's numbers, there was a big lesson out of him working with Alex: a successful collaboration could begin with something as simple as "Hey, let's meet up."

That kind of positive reinforcement encouraged—no, forced—Nash to be outgoing. Knowing there were all kinds of opportunities out there made him want to be more open and communicative.

I'm not saying it was always easy, but I pushed myself to reach out whenever I could. Soon enough, collaboration became part of the fabric of my being.

Nash even got an idea to start a collab page on Vine, taking his inspiration from a collab page on YouTube that was blowing up. He got everyone together that had been at MagCon for that collab page, where they could constantly post and keep people updated. They all brought their different strengths, communities, and social media platforms together. So where one guy had a ton of Instagram followers, because that's how he got his start, another one was big on YouTube. Even when two of them were big on the same site, there were variations that drove different audiences—like Shawn Mendes and Nash, who were both big on Vine, except Shawn came from the music scene, whereas Nash was more comedy.

WITH SHAWN MENDES AT THE MTV
VIDEO MUSIC AWARDS IN 2015

The point is, there were some really cool, successful people on that collab page, people who were going to change the world. Their continued growth showed in the second MagCon that they attended, which was held in Orlando. It was on the heels of the first meet and greet, but the number of people who bought tickets for this event was considerably bigger. In Dallas they had 2,000 people show up and in Orlando it was more like 4,000 or 5,000. Their compensation went up, too; this time the organizers gave each participant $500 and a pair of Beats headphones.

Even though they were selling thousands of tickets for about $125, we didn't know any better. We were just hyped to hang out—and for the Beats.

By the third MagCon, in Washington, D.C.—which happened to overlap with Nash's sixteenth birthday, on December 28, 2013—he began to question the economics of the whole business of social media and whether or not he could actually make a career of it. This was a radical idea. First of all, just a few months prior he was dead set on playing college lacrosse and put almost every waking moment that he wasn't in class into that goal. But that seemed like a million years ago. Before he started making viral videos in a twenty-four-year-old's car. Before he started flying around the country to meet and hug thousands of fans.

Use every experience as an opportunity to learn and you'll never waste your time.

So Nash started talking to his dad and mom about it. Could this be a career? If so, what exactly was this career? And should he do it, even if it was real? He didn't know what attracted him to the idea the most. Was it the self-empowering aspect, in that anyone could create content and get it out there? Or was it the interactive piece, that the content Nash made could touch as many people as he had met in Dallas or Orlando—or more? Or was it the fact that his videos could be a way to be creative?

My mom had said, "Do whatever your heart says. . . . It's your life." Unfortunately in this case, I wasn't sure what my heart was saying.

Nash needed his parents' help. After they all started to talk about the future, he wanted them to understand what this whole thing was about. "Guys, you have to see for yourself," he said, because they had no idea what was going on. So they went with him to D.C. to experience for themselves what Nash had described.

Well, Nash's parents might not have been that impressed by the fact that at this point he was the second-most-followed person in the world on Vine, with more than 4.6 million followers, had 870,000 on Twitter, and 1.89 million on Instagram, but boy, were they bowled over by seeing all those MagCon attendees in D.C. and how the fans reacted to their middle son. They realized there was potential for Nash to have a big impact. Still, the path was not at all clear. So throughout MagCon, the family continued to have conversations. They circled around the same questions over and over.

"What is this?"

"What is going on?"

"What am I doing?"

Focus your energy on doing what's right, not what's easy.

It was within this context of confusion and exploration that Nash decided to go for his next big opportunity—a trip to Iceland!

Like everything else, this unbelievable adventure came totally out of the blue and it came superfast.

If there's a defining moment in my life this is it.

While Nash was still in D.C., a live-stream app contacted him about flying to Iceland for a week to act as an ambassador to promote their new product. So in January 2014 he took off for an eleven-day, life-changing trip—with his grandma.

My dad's mom, Carol, whom I call Mimi, always traveled with me whenever neither of my parents could. She loved it, because she loves to travel. And I loved it because she's awesome and very high-spirited.

The other person Nash traveled to Iceland with was Jerome Jarre, a twenty-three-year-old French Vine star and business entrepreneur.

And really cool guy.

His story is pretty amazing. He was born and raised by a single mom in Albertville, a small country town in the Alps where he was bullied a lot because of his shyness. That's ironic since Jerome's confidence and outgoing spirit took him to places and to meet people those bullies in Albertville couldn't dream of.

When Jerome was nineteen, he left his home, dropped out of business school, and moved all the way to China. That takes some serious guts. He wound up living there for a year, learning to speak English *and* Chinese, and started about a half dozen businesses. But none of them worked out. When he bought a one-way bus ticket from Canada, where he'd been living after China, to New York in 2013, he only had $400. *Total.* In one of the most expensive cities in the world, Jerome survived by sleeping in an office and sneaking into a gym to shower!

But he was also making Vines, which turned out to be a gold mine for him. Jerome is the definition of an early adopter. He posted his first Vine the day the site launched. He and Nash shared a similar style; Jerome also did funny videos and harmless pranks, like one where he says into the camera "Why is everybody afraid of love?" Then he runs up to some poor unsuspecting woman shopping in a supermarket and scares the crap out of her by shouting "Love!" Good stuff. So good, Ellen DeGeneres had Jerome on as a guest on her popular TV show, where he told her that his Vines didn't make everyone happy. Once he was chased by a baseball bat–wielding truck driver after Jerome woke the driver up while making a video.

Most people, however, did love his Vines, and Jerome launched to the fourth-most-popular spot on Vine, behind

Nash and two other comedians, King Bach and Brittany Furlan. It wasn't his Vine ranking that really impressed Nash. A few months before they met, Jerome started a totally rad Vine project, Humans, where he asked strangers "What is the most important message you would like to share with the world right now?" Now, that's a good use of tech.

Don't waste your time with what you hate, focus your energy on what you love.

Nash was psyched to be traveling to such a different place as Iceland with someone as thoughtful and interesting as Jerome. But he had never been out of the country before, and so he didn't know what to expect.

You don't know what's out in the world until you go into it yourself.

Well, one thing they did was crash the app he was supposed to be in the country to promote. The servers could not hold the amount of people that they brought on to live-stream. It just didn't have the bandwidth to support all their followers. Jerome and Nash were psyched to get such a warm reception in Iceland, but the purpose of their trip was crushed since they couldn't live-stream from the app.

The company reps were just like "Oh well. Enjoy the trip."

And they did. They hung out and had fun, traveling to the glaciers and waterfalls that dot Iceland's beautiful landscape. Still, no matter what they were doing, they were also making videos.

Constantly.

Jerome and Nash joined forces making content and posting it together. This was right around when Nash started making his YouTube channel a real thing, sending his followers from Vine over to other sites by asking them to "check this video out" or "come follow me on here." He started on Vine but actively spread it out on YouTube, Twitter, and Instagram, so that he was rapidly growing everywhere.

Because Nash had seen the quick effect of his calls to action, he shouldn't have been surprised by the popular reception they received in Iceland. But he totally was.

On January 4, Jerome and Nash announced a meet-up at a mall in Kópavogur, a municipality just south of Reykjavik, Iceland's capital and largest city. Although Nash had done meet and greets at MagCon, he had never done a meet-up where he just kind of put it out there. He wasn't sure how he felt about it, but Jerome made a picture for him to post, which Nash did on Twitter. It didn't say much more than "Come say hi to us today at 4 p.m. at the mall."

They chose the mall on purpose, because they wanted to do a free meet-up, where they didn't have to book a venue or hire security. Well, that turned out to be a big mistake. BIG.

Jerome and Nash had imagined a casual event with a pretty small crowd. Iceland as a whole isn't a big place, and they didn't think too many people would show up in the middle of the afternoon at a mall to see anyone—let alone them.

They couldn't have been more wrong. Six thousand teenagers showed up for their meet-up!

It was insane. The mall was so packed, you couldn't even walk. Suddenly I found myself drowning in a sea of people all speaking Icelandic. I tried to locate Jerome visually, but he was on another level of the mall. It was hopeless.

The mob swept up Nash, who ended up getting pushed into a shop where the owner let him go through the back into an inner corridor. So Nash escaped being crushed to death by thousands of Icelandic fans, but now he was in a corridor in a mall in Iceland with no cell phone service. Even worse, he didn't know what had happened to Grandma!

As he made his way down the corridor as if he were in a spoof of *Mission: Impossible,* he thought, *There's no way I'm getting out of here.* But then he found a door, pushed it open, and it led outside! He started running, although to where, he wasn't sure. It didn't take long before he saw Jerome, who was on top of a car, *Mad Max*–style, telling everybody to calm down.

The parking lot outside was just as chaotic as inside the mall. There were thousands of people running, pushing, climbing on cars—you know, your garden-variety riot.

This might not have been the biggest deal in the United States (although it probably would have made some kind of news). But in Iceland, things like this didn't happen, ever.

The narrative of every news outlet in Iceland following our meet-up was that the country hadn't seen anything like it since the Beatles!

The mall, which only had one security guard on duty at the time, was overrun. People who didn't know about the meet-up—including the security guard—were panicked, thinking that it might be some kind of terrorist attack. Even Jerome, who like Nash had expected about twenty people to show, admitted to the media that he had been really scared.

The police force arrived on the scene to put an end to the chaos about a half hour later. Guys in flak jackets and helmets, with walkie-talkies and guns, started emptying the mall of people—and found Nash's grandma.

Thanks, Icelandic SWAT team!

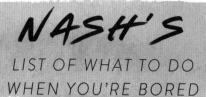

NASH'S
LIST OF WHAT TO DO
WHEN YOU'RE BORED

- Go tubing

- Build a tree house

- Build a fort out of sheets

- Build a slip-and-slide with a tarp, soap, and a hose

- Paint

- Stand on your head and hands

- Meditate

- Look through a telescope

CHAPTER 5

Nash looked out at the fluffy clouds and bright blue sky, but mentally he was a million miles away. For most of the six-hour plane ride from Iceland back to the States, he stayed glued to the window, where his thoughts could roam freely.

Some of it was reflection. What a trip! The mall visit alone had resulted in a few minor injuries and damages to some of the parked cars—enough so that Jerome posted an apology on Twitter and vowed never to do a meet-up without real security again.

Thank God, Mimi, my grandma, came out of it without so much as a scratch.

Mostly, Nash was trying to process what the heck was happening to him. Dallas. Orlando. D.C. Iceland. Each one was an experience more extreme than the last—and all of it from these little scenes caught on video, or random thoughts in his head sent

GAME DAY IN WEST VIRGINIA WITH HAYES AND MIMI

from his phone to millions of peers out there wanting to, needing to, connect in some way.

The same questions he had been mulling over continued to churn in his brain. *What could this be? Do I want to do this, whatever this is? Can I create a new life?*

On the plane ride home, all these thoughts crystallized into a choice. Did Nash want to stick with what he'd been doing so far, finish the path he had chosen for himself at Davidson Day, with lacrosse and college? Or did he want to go for . . . go for . . . go for what?

Plan A was definitive: finishing high school and going to college. You can't get much more solid than that. Plan B wasn't even really a plan, because Nash couldn't name what it was. So Plan A it was. That's what he was going to do.

As the plane touched down, there was not a doubt in his mind. This whole crazy adventure had been cool. And sure, he could see the impact his social media presence was having on thousands of people when they stormed a mall to meet him. The fact that he had something to say that could energize six thousand people, nothing could compare to that. But, no, Plan A. That was the only thing that really existed.

Except it wasn't.

As Nash gained more followers and more attention, so grew his drive to create better content. He wanted to make his videos funnier, more interesting, just better. And to do that he had to spend more time making them.

He started waking up before school and filming for hours. This was before the technology had caught up to the medium, and it was impossible to edit the videos he posted to Vine. At the time, the app didn't have a function for editing, so you basically had to do everything in one take.

I'd literally shoot something, pause, shoot something else, pause, and, if I messed up the third shot, I'd have to reshoot the first shot, second, and third again. If I messed up the fifth shot . . . I had to start all over again.

It was *very* time-consuming. Or at least it could be. Some Vines took just minutes to make, like a classic of Skylynn singing

"Boom Boom Pow" by the Black Eyed Peas. Three minutes of production resulted in 375,000 likes and 300,000 re-Vines. But then again, Skylynn's a star.

Others took him hours and hours to make. Usually the most interesting six-second stories from the long list of ideas

—which came to me wherever and whenever and that I kept on my iPhone—

were the hardest to accomplish. In one of his more high-adventure and action-oriented Vines, Nash yelled "shotgun," claiming the front seat of the car, then ran, swam, and skateboarded to get to the seat. That was a nightmare to get right.

When the sun was just coming up for the day, hours before the first school bell was set to ring, he was cameraman, actor, and editor all rolled into one. He was also CEO of his own brand.

Not that I had any idea what that meant.

He had to make sure he could get the most eyeballs and impressions on his stuff, attract the most followers that week, and see how many times he could repeat that process. Basically, Nash had to post something that got on the top of the popular page on Vine every single day.

He learned by trial and error, because how else could he figure this stuff out?

A loss can be a lesson.

There was no model or formula to follow, no one to teach him. It wasn't like he had someone telling him what to do. It was just him, alone in his head. He needed to earn followers the best he could. By tweaking the times he posted, Nash got the knack of driving traffic directly to his videos down to a science. The process went like this: wait until everybody on the East Coast is three hours out of school, and when everyone on the West Coast is just getting out of school. That's when you post. That way, you have as many kids at once on their phones checking out what's new on social media as possible. And you gotta keep it consistent, so people get conditioned to look for something new.

Everything was very scheduled and organized, which is usually the case with anyone who makes it big. There were some six-second videos Nash made that have four million likes or replays, which humbled him. The fact that four million people took the time to watch something he made, let alone replay it, never lost its thrill.

Nash started to get this funny feeling, like he was entering uncharted territory. He could tell that he owned the space he was in. As far as he could tell, nobody else was thinking about this stuff—and even if they were, they weren't doing it like he was. He had scoured the internet to see who else was in this universe and who was at the top of it. Then he tried to extrapolate from their examples the secrets to their accomplishments. No one could deny the numbers; his analytics were working.

It felt really, really cool to know as much as I knew about my audience and about how things worked. Kind of like how I felt when I discovered lacrosse, this was something that was all mine. Even my parents had trouble understanding what was going on.

From the perspective of the internet, Nash watched the entire world change. He was there before social media became popular; before posting was the norm; before selfies became a real thing; before any of that existed; before businesses or people spent money on influencers online.

That was another thing Nash educated himself on—the business of being a social media personality. After he saw that other social media kids had a business email account and sites with their bios and other professional information, he created an official bio for himself with a business email. When he returned from Iceland, the inquiries and offers from agencies, start-ups, and big businesses continued to heat up. Everyone seemed to want to work with him, although he knew they had no idea who he was or what he could bring to the table.

Even the meet and greets that he was already doing got considerably more lucrative. The next one Nash was offered was in Nashville, and instead of $500 and a pair of Beats headphones, they were paying an up-front fee of around $2,000!

Back when he had first started making videos, he instantly got taken advantage of on the business side. That pretty often happens to people just starting out, but it is particularly likely when you're a teen and the business you're in is still being invented.

Nash would have kept letting it happen, especially when it came to the meet and greets, because he had never been happier than when he was meeting all those people. It was a rush (and then depleting afterward) to encounter so many excited human beings in one place.

The $2,000 paycheck wasn't just an issue of fairness. That amount of money was significant for Nash's family, which like so many other families in America had been struggling ever since the financial crisis of 2008. In the ensuing recession, his stepdad lost his job, and his dad wasn't making consistent money, either. They didn't struggle as much as others, folks who didn't have food or other basic necessities. Still, his parents struggled to maintain the lifestyle they wanted to give Nash and his brothers. For example, playing lacrosse was really expensive. On top of tuition for Davidson Day, there was a $3,000 fee for the equipment, travel, etc.

As much as I loved the sport, I felt bad because I knew how hard it was for my mom to pay that.

With money definitely an issue at this point, whenever Nash earned $250 for a post or $2,000 for a meet and greet, it was significant. It meant he could do stuff without bugging his parents for cash—like buying a good lunch for school.

I know that might sound stupid, but when you're at school from 8 a.m. to 8 p.m., as I was for lacrosse, food means a lot. Every day I packed so much food it was insane—breakfast, lunch, and something to eat for later. I would have the biggest lunches Davidson Day had ever seen—you can ask anyone. But when I got a little cash, the first thing I'd do is sneak out of school (because only seniors were allowed to go off campus) and go to one of the restaurants right across the street to buy lunch. My favorite place was Char-Grill, where I'd order a burger with a fried egg on top. Amazing stuff. I'd come back to school, where everyone else had their lunch that'd been sitting in their bags all day, and I had this delicious, hot food. Man, were the other kids jealous.

When Nash returned from Iceland, it was such a strange time, full of contradictions, experimentation, soul-searching, a quickly changing online landscape, and so, so much work. Every day, more and more people were creating new social media accounts, which only added to what Nash was already doing. His follow count on everything was shooting through the roof. New requests were coming at all times. If he wasn't editing or shooting, Nash was posting.

Nowadays, people are on their phones so much, that in a way their virtual and real lives are always connected. Social media affects your actions, and vice versa. But at the time Nash was coming up on Vine, YouTube, and other sites, social media and reality were two totally different worlds. For Nash, it was hard to reconcile the two. As he tried to live his life as a normal kid, more and more he was met with abnormal responses because of what he was doing on the internet.

There was the issue of people recognizing him wherever he went. It didn't matter if he was at the supermarket with his mom, at a football game for Will, or a restaurant with his dad. He was always getting bombarded by people who wanted pictures. Posing for one photo turned into two more, which turned into a mob. He couldn't eat dinner with his family out in public. He couldn't do anything.

But the real trouble with trying to be normal *and* a social media star was school. The more class time he missed, the harder it became for him to keep up with his courses.

In the area outside the dean of students office, near a few other administrative offices, there was a little table where kids had to sit if they had detention or were behind on their class assignments for any reason. They basically went to this table after school and sat there for hours doing their work without any kind of distraction. That became Nash's spot at Davidson Day. At his first enforced study hall, faced with heaps of unfinished school-work, he grew very dispirited. There wasn't just a pile for one subject—but one for each and every class he had!

Nash found himself in that classic vicious cycle that kids get into when they fall behind. When you miss class, you don't understand the work, so you can't do it. Then you just fall further behind, because you don't understand the classes that build on the work you didn't do in the first place.

I took all these packets home and tried to teach myself the lesson, but I didn't get too far.

Davidson Day does its best to work with its students to make sure that nobody falls behind on account of the school. They are very flexible and will accommodate students who have outside professional careers.

The school once had a student who was a race-car driver.

For Nash, though, he felt like he could either focus on school or he couldn't. There was no denying something huge was taking his focus away from his education.

In general, that's the kind of person I am. I need to be doing one thing. It can involve a bunch of little things, but overall everything needs to be moving toward the same point or focus. I hate being all over the place, having half of my mind here and the other half over there. I like a clean slate, so I can make decisions. Otherwise everything just feels like a waste of time.

Sitting at the table outside the dean's office with a big pile of work in front of him—when he had just come back from Iceland—Nash couldn't help but ask himself over and over, "Why am I doing this?"

This wasn't Nash's first experience chafing at the rigidity of school. When he was a little kid at elementary school, he'd cry his eyes out on Sundays, saying to his mom, "I don't want to go to school." He would do anything to get out of going to school. Little Nash just hated it. Not because he hated learning. On the contrary, he loved learning and always has.

Knowledge is power, for sure. But on whose terms?

No matter which of the many schools he went to, Nash couldn't cope whenever he had a teacher who didn't stray from the textbook or showed passion only when proving that they know way more than everyone else sitting in the classroom.

You know, the let-me-just-shove-this-down-your-throat method of teaching. I need a teacher I can really have a dialogue with.

The only teacher at Nash's school that he felt like he could really talk to was Ms. Brown. In her class, AP biology, he had the most homework. But because she engaged him as a fellow human being and not some kind of information slave, he always managed to get it done. Nash would actually spend hours in her classroom just doing schoolwork, because her class was, no question, his favorite. They would do real hands-on stuff toward the study of life. Not only did she take her students through the basics of living organisms, but she also took them on field trips to lakes and paleontological sites. Ms. Brown gauged their interests, and instead of being annoyed by them, she used their sense of curiosity as a jumping-off point. But Ms. Brown was the exception.

I hate being told what to do—and what to learn.
Environments where that's the normal way things
function don't work for me. I love communication,
give-and-take, and gaining wisdom. But commands? No
thanks. So in that way, I always felt that school
was my enemy.

As the month of January dragged on, Nash began to doubt everything. His worlds were no doubt colliding, but neither world was prevailing as the clear winner of the competition. He could see the good and bad in each situation. Yes, school was a bummer right now. Between the kids at school, not being there enough to keep up with his schoolwork because of meet and greets and other events, and losing the thread of the curriculum, Nash felt like he couldn't take it anymore. But then again, he did have a teacher like Ms. Brown to get him through. Then he'd go to a great college and be set. But set for what? His posts and videos were touching people all over the world, which was beyond amazing. But what could he do with that? Nash really wanted to develop in his own unique way, which school was not conducive toward.

Nash was all over the place. He could see all the dots, but he couldn't connect them himself. He needed someone or something to show him how. He was having so much trouble figuring out what was going to happen to him, or what he wanted to happen to him. He wanted one part of his life to rise up above the other in importance. He wanted a sign to show him that one path was the right one to take.

Then, in the last week of January 2014, he got it.

Nash was offered the opportunity to be the live digital presence at the 56th Annual Grammy Awards in Los Angeles! He was going to tweet and post to other sites from the red carpet, which in itself was a once-in-a-lifetime experience. But his dad, always thinking of the long game, decided to use the trip out to L.A. for greater purposes.

It was Nash's first time to L.A. and, honestly, he was ready to explode. He just wanted a direction and a hard push toward it.

For the last couple of weeks I had been too much in my head, but the way my dad planned the week we spent on the West Coast—I didn't have time to think at all.

Chad set up at least twenty meetings that he packed into the five business days he and Nash were in town before the Grammys. Every day, starting at 8 a.m. and going until 6 p.m.—when they returned to the hotel and basically collapsed from exhaustion—father and son were either sitting in a meeting, driving to a meeting, or setting another meeting up. The week out in L.A. with his dad wasn't unlike the team training trips to the mountains Chad led as his football coach. There was no downtime.

The question they set out to answer with that trip was whether Nash's stardom on social media actually meant anything real. Where could he take his online presence, and did it have long-term prospects? Or was this just his fifteen minutes of fame? Because there was no model for them to look at on how to monetize his social media success, they had to go out there and do the research themselves by talking to a whole host of people.

Nash and his dad met with talent agencies to see what that was all about. Marketers, production-company heads, entertainment media brand executives, people who manage YouTube channels—they all explained what they did, how Nash could build on what he had already achieved and grow it even bigger. They insisted that what he had experienced was only the tip of the iceberg. Nash got a real education, and so did his dad, which was very important. Not only did Nash have to get permission from Chad if he wanted to go off and explore this life as an option, but he also trusted that his father had the life experience to know whether this was just his fifteen minutes.

That was the crucial part of the trip, although there was one other little part to it, which was the Grammys. Nash got a front-row seat to the biggest night in music with the coolest people, like Justin Timberlake, Kendrick Lamar, and Macklemore.

I even snapped a pic with Pharrell Williams while he was sporting that insane ranger hat on steroids.

When Nash returned home from California, there was no more delaying his decision. He had missed so much school now that he was really beginning to jeopardize his Plan A—to use lacrosse and his extracurricular activities as a way to get into college. If he wanted to finish Davidson Day, he had to cut way back on his social media stuff—and if he was going to do that, then he didn't want to do it at all.

BACK HOME FROM L.A.

But the universe took its course and set him on a whole other trajectory. When Nash wanted to quit football to try something else, his mom encouraged him to go for whatever he dreamed up, to make his life what he wanted it to be. When Nash returned from L.A., he realized his dreams were what he was already doing.

You can depend on whatever and whoever you want for happiness but deep down if you can make yourself happy, life becomes much easier.

That was the moment when Nash made one of the hardest decisions of his life: to drop out of school, move across the country to Los Angeles, and figure out how to make this thing real.

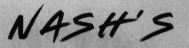

NASH'S

BUCKET LIST
(in no particular order of importance)

- Grow enough food to live off of
- Build a house
- Write and direct a feature film
- Star in someone's passion project
- Drive across America
- Be active as a senior
- Explore the ocean in a submarine
- Plant a forest
- Skydive
- Watch the Panthers win the Super Bowl
- Help end water crisis
- Give a platform to all those in need
- Create an animal rescue
- Raise a happy family

CHAPTER 6

Nash's dad cried the whole way to the airport. Chad Grier, the toughest high school football coach in North Carolina, was crying his eyes out. When they finally got to the terminal where they had to say goodbye, Nash lost it, too. How could he not? Taking off for Los Angeles to live on his own at sixteen was emotionally and mentally the most challenging thing he'd ever done.

Nash had made up his mind that this is what he wanted. Months earlier, he had decided it was time to stop attending Davidson Day and instead focus on trying to make a career out of his social media full-time. He recognized it was a major risk.

Although to be honest, lacrosse as a career path was no better. It was going to be an uphill, probably losing battle for me to get into an Ivy League school, since my academics had suffered with the rise of my online fame. And even if I made it to the upper echelons of professional lacrosse, that did not ensure any kind of stability. Because there's no lacrosse on TV, people who play the sport professionally basically have to work three jobs to survive. It's brutal.

Still back home, Nash had wanted to see how far he could take this thing. That's when he started to really dig in to his videos for his YouTube channel. If Nash wasn't filming or editing, he was writing—mini scripts, new ideas, single words that would jog the entire creative process.

That's also when he developed a full presentation to convince his parents why they should let him leave school and move across the country to pursue a dream. This wasn't an easy sell, so Nash had to be professional, thorough, and persuasive.

"All right. This is what's going to happen." He pitched his parents as if he were in a meeting full of Hollywood agents. "I will enroll in one of these five online schools where I can keep up with my grade level. That way if my career in California doesn't work out, I can come home instantly and finish school as if I had never left at all."

Nash set it up so that they couldn't say no, because he wasn't going to take any answer other than yes.

Of course, they could and *did* say no. Nash's timing wasn't great. His parents had been prepared for his older brother, Will, to leave, but no sooner had he left for college than Nash was declaring he was out, too. Understandably, they needed some time to wrap their heads around having two of their boys leave the nest so close to one another.

Once I make up my mind about what I want to do, there is no getting me off it.

Nash gave that presentation to his mom and/or dad so much he had it memorized. It became almost a normal part of his everyday routine, like brushing his teeth.

Whether they were sick of listening to him or actually believed in him, after a couple of months of wearing them down, Nash got his parents' consent.

I like to think they agreed I was doing the right thing by moving to L.A., that I was following my instincts and what I was meant to do.

The truth is Nash's parents wouldn't let him go to L.A. until he had a "real" reason to be there. In this case, it was a part in a feature film—Nash's acting debut! Although the deal wasn't officially announced until months later. Fullscreen, a big YouTube network, was launching a division devoted to films, and one of its first projects, *The Outfield*, was set to star Cameron Dallas and Nash.

If Nash appeared confident about his future when he pitched his parents his plan, as soon as he got on that plane to California, he was anything but.

I'm so glad my parents made me wait to get there.

Although leaving home felt like it was supposed to happen, it didn't necessarily feel *right*. It wasn't like Nash was running away from a bad situation at home. Even though his parents had been divorced since he was five, each of them still played an important role in his life every single day, which he assumed they would to continue to do until he went to college.

But as unnatural as it felt when his dad left him at the airport, this was the right thing to do. There was no other way; Nash had to say goodbye and walk away from everything he had known his entire life until that point.

For the duration of the plane ride, he was totally exhausted. The whole emotional aspect of deciding to separate from his family was so much for him. But even more overwhelming was that as hard as this all was, *this* was just the start. As soon as Nash touched down on the other side of the country, he wasn't going to have anyone on his team. Even when he met people out in California, they weren't necessarily going to be on his side.

How do you meet people in L.A.?

How do you even live there?

How do you not get screwed over?

How do you not have the tallest walls, ever, around yourself?

I didn't know the first thing about anything.

In that moment up in the sky, it hit him. At sixteen, Nash made a decision, which was "All right. Time to grow up. Let's just take on the world."

FIRST APARTMENT IN L.A. (PEEP MY HIGHLIGHTS)

The first challenge presented itself before Nash even took one step inside his new apartment.

As soon as he pulled up to the building on North La Brea at Hollywood Boulevard, there were two hundred girls waiting for him outside his front door! He hadn't even moved in yet, and they already knew he was there. If Nash thought having students at Davidson Day always trying to video him at school, or people back home in North Carolina asking for pictures was challenging—this was forty thousand times harder. The paparazzi, the people, the flashbulbs going off in his eyes, the yelling, the pushing.

Fame is as simple as others treating you differently. Learning to cope with it is a lot more complicated.

Not a single day went by that there weren't fans or paparazzi waiting outside the apartment, which he shared with his Mag-Con comrade Cam Dallas. It was a two-bedroom duplex, with one bedroom on the top floor, which Cam took, and another one Nash slept in, on the bottom floor, where the kitchen and living room also were.

Cam and Nash were the first people from the original Mag-Con group who relocated to L.A. While everyone else was still debating college, they believed that social media was actually worth something. It didn't take long for the rest of the guys to follow them out there. Thanks to fans like those hanging outside their place, their social media presence was nonstop. Every single day, Nash's following would generate new content by taking pictures, making videos, or interacting in ways that blew up Nash and his crew. The energy was incredible.

Nash's online life was bananas. But his real life on earth couldn't have been more different. It was kind of like a prisoner's. When he first moved out to L.A., Nash was strictly monitored. He had to call his father at eight o'clock every single morning. If he wasn't on the phone with his dad by that time, something was wrong. One time, Nash missed a day, and Chad was out there the very next morning.

That's not an exaggeration. It was without warning. I almost had a heart attack when I woke up, because there he was, standing over me. "Oh god!!!" was all I could say. Chad Grier does not play.

Nash had persuaded his parents to let him move to L.A. but they made all the rules. It didn't matter that their son was more than two thousand miles away. He was still sixteen years old, and that meant he had to do things like homework and be home by midnight. But just in case they couldn't maintain their grip on Nash from thousands of miles away, they hired someone to live in the apartment and keep an eye on him.

They didn't just hire anyone—it was the world's strongest man.

Literally. I'm not kidding.

Ralph was a power lifter who had broken international records in the sport, which earned him the title of "world's strongest man." He was like a four-hundred-pound gorilla-man. Just ginormous. And he promised Chad, "I'm going to keep Nash safe." Part bodyguard, part nanny, Ralph meant well and was ultimately a good guy. But he was annoying. He cooked the grossest food, made the corniest jokes, and kept them from having any fun—not that there was much time in Nash's schedule for fun, anyway.

Nash's first manager was a guy who chain-smoked everywhere, including in the car while they were off to take one of the million meetings he had set up. He filled up every waking minute of every day of every week of Nash's life.

Each day began with four hours of acting classes. At least. Nash worked with two teachers, Deb Aquila and Marjorie Ballentine, both of whom are very talented and experienced. They are also both protégés of the famed acting teacher Stella Adler, whose technique encouraged the imagination and internal psychological and emotional qualities over external devices. It produced such legendary actors as Marlon Brando and Robert De Niro. Deb, who graduated from New York University's Tisch School of the Arts and the Stella Adler Conservatory, isn't only an acting coach but also a casting director who has cast hundreds of movies and TV shows. Marjorie, a coach and theater director, has worked with a wide range of actors from the big screen to Broadway, including Gary Oldman and Krysten Ritter.

You get the picture; this wasn't Ms. Gertie's improv class at Davidson Day.

Nash had a lot to learn. After his four hours of classes in a little auditorium with twenty people and a teacher, he'd usually sit in on the master class to watch the more advanced students at work—if he wasn't doing one-on-one sessions with one of the coaches.

And that was just the start of the day! Nash was also posting stuff to his various accounts, taking meetings while smelling like an ashtray after riding with his then manager, and then spending upward of twelve hours on set making videos for his YouTube channel.

As soon as he moved out to L.A., Nash started making full-on skits with a crew and everything. This was as far as you could get from his start running across his lawn fifty times until he got each second right for a Vine. They shot high-quality, high-production stuff. Nash had his own director and his own set, although sometimes they shot in his apartment, where there could be twenty people and all their equipment crammed into the kitchen and living room. Wherever they took place, Nash was proud of the videos they were making, all of which got at least five million views on YouTube.

But for every two hours of filming he did, Nash had to do an hour of schoolwork. That was the legal educational requirement, because of the fact that he was not yet eighteen. It was nothing for him to spend eight to ten hours shooting, and then another four to five hours on top of that with a tutor. His online courses weren't any easier or more convenient. Nash found teaching himself the courses frustrating, and submitting the work time-consuming. It took hours just to hand in one assignment.

School ended up not working out for Nash. It would have been different if he believed in its purpose and end goal, but he just didn't, and he couldn't lie to himself.

The first thing you have to teach a kid is the desire to learn. If you don't want to learn, you can't absorb anything. You've got to teach them about things that are so interesting and cool, they want to read or research more about them beyond the parameters of the assignment. If the subject matter is engaging enough and the classroom environment stimulating, then students will want to do homework, return to their peers with something new to add, and take the lead in their own learning. There are schools like that—places that first

> open kids up to ideas, which in turn opens up doors
> for them. If I could have gone to one, I would
> have been all for it. But I didn't have that kind
> of time or opportunity in L.A.

Nash was in California to create a career for himself, and, frankly, formal schooling didn't have any place in that plan.

Nash ended up not finishing high school online like he had initially planned, but instead took the GED.

> I don't believe that a piece of paper should
> determine your worth or your value. At the same
> time, I do believe it kind of does, since society says
> it does. If the world says you need that piece of
> paper to get a job, then you actually have to go
> get it. And that sucks, but you do.

He also had to prove to his parents that he wasn't going rogue in L.A. Nash needed to have the most basic form of diploma he could get, or his dad would be on the first flight out there to pack him up and take him home (probably unannounced).

So Nash told himself, "I'll just be safe and get a GED." That's exactly what he did, but there was something in that kind of safety that bummed him out. It also hinted at a larger problem he was having when he first moved to L.A.

His first four months in California were rough. They were probably the hardest ones of his life. It wasn't the work. He didn't mind being busy.

> *I've always worked hard (I'm my dad's son after all),*
> *and I definitely didn't come to L.A. to sit around.*

He loved all he was learning about the digital space—from taking pictures with happy fans to acting and meeting new people who opened him up to new business and life opportunities.

Part of the difficulty had to do with the fact that he was adjusting to a whole new rhythm of life on his own. First there were his physical surroundings.

> *I went from the woods to Hollywood Boulevard,*
> *where it's not unusual to see people lying facedown*
> *on the concrete. I couldn't understand why nobody*
> *cared somebody was passed out on the ground.*

L.A. was a lonely place in a lot of ways. Nash was surrounded by a lot of people—at acting class, on set, in meetings. But he had never felt more isolated. Especially in the apartment, where he did *not* count Ralph as companionship. If Cam was working, Nash didn't have any friends around. Feeling completely isolated, after being raised in a big family, was very difficult.

> *If I found myself alone for a whole weekend or*
> *week, because Cam was traveling, it took a toll on*
> *my head.*

Not having anyone overseeing him but himself was also a weird freedom to have so young. The whole freedom of being on your own, making your own decisions, being your own person, is something people, especially if they're young, are usually eased into. It's not something they wake up to one day after taking a five-hour flight across the country. He didn't even know how to get his own food. Every single day: breakfast, lunch, and dinner? *Um, all right. That shouldn't be too hard.* That's what he thought, but it was hard—at least for him, as a sixteen-year-old.

I ate like crap. It was gas station food nonstop and a lot of Subway. I couldn't cook to save my life. Laundry wasn't much better, either.

But it wasn't soggy foot-long sandwiches that were bringing Nash down. It wasn't even really so much being alone. As he contemplated his situation, he knew he didn't need any more attention. He had plenty of that. He had directors, managers, agents, lawyers, and other people talking to him, telling him what to do, providing him with a structure to his day, his work, and his life—so much that he couldn't escape from it.

"This is what you need to be out here."

"This is what you need to be doing."

"This is your schedule."

"This is your next twelve hours."

That's all Nash heard.

And he did everything they said to do. Just like getting his GED, Nash was doing it to be safe. He was working his butt off, every single day, and doing it for all these people who only saw him as an opportunity.

I felt important, but I didn't feel wanted. It's easy to feel important and not feel wanted.

The result was Nash out in Los Angeles, living his "dream" with every resource at his fingertips, and feeling utterly unmotivated.

He couldn't make sense of what was happening or how to fix it. All he knew was that, as he moved through the endless cycle of working, studying, coming home, eating, sleeping, working, studying . . . he started to feel really low. *Did I make the wrong decision by doing this?* he wondered. *I'm just not happy.*

NASH'S

 French Polynesia

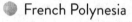 Georgia (the country)

Brazil

CHAPTER 7

Slowly, the rest of the MagCon crew started to make their way out west.

Jack & Jack, Dylan, Sammy Wilkinson, Skate. One guy came out, then another.

They were all new to the city and living there, just like Nash. Quickly, that number jumped to ten. Some of their families came out too—sisters, brothers, more friends—and together, they became a tribe.

Away from home, they were all trying to find themselves and their place, while making connections and getting stuff done. The experiment was to see if these young people could work *and* have fun. Nash felt like he needed—and deserved—both sides of life. He wasn't going to be able to make a career for himself in

California if he wasn't allowed to have a good time. But what did it mean to "have a good time"?

His original manny, Ralph, was a good guy, who only wanted the best for him. Nash knew that.

He was trying to keep me on track and in focus, but I hated that he was in my face.

But Ralph had to go. Their chemistry was off. *Way off.* Nash associated him with a dark transition time. So with his dad's approval, Nash got to pick the next guardian to live with him and Cam—and he chose Yosh.

The coolest guy ever.

Yosh was a friend of theirs whom they hired sometimes to accompany Nash when he traveled for meet and greets or other things that took him on the road. Yosh was always that guy who connected with Chad to let him know that "Nash is safe." So he seemed like a perfect choice to come live with Nash, and Chad thankfully agreed.

Nash loved Yosh's vibe.

Yosh, the sweetest guy in the world, he knew when to be funny and when to be serious. When he stepped into that role of our bodyguard, that's when the creative environment got amazing. He treated us like adults.

The one bad thing about Yosh, though, was he smoked cigarettes. A lot of cigarettes.

"Yosh, that's not good for you, man," Nash said when Yosh lit up his millionth cigarette of the day. "You can't be doing that. How about we make a bet on you quitting? We can bet money; we can bet whatever. But let's just bet something."

They ended up not really betting, but instead doing a vegetarian versus no-tobacco dare. Nash had been talking a lot about wanting to

WITH JACK J. IN A RANDOM GAS STATION. I CAN'T EXPLAIN THIS ONE.

give up meat, but he never seemed to find the right time. Well, according to Yosh, no time like the present. For the entire four months they lived together, he didn't smoke, and Nash didn't eat meat. It was life-changing for both of them. Nash felt good energy and all that nice stuff. Yosh was able to breathe without coughing.

As far as I know, Yosh never started smoking cigarettes again. Either way, I definitely loved that guy.

Nash continued to work as hard as ever, making videos and getting new projects off the ground.

We worked so hard and partied just as hard.

Nash had no problem meeting people. He met people on the internet and at events revolving around social media all the time. There were thousands upon thousands of new folks at his fingertips. They might have begun as contacts on the screen, but soon enough, they became real faces and sometimes friends—at least that's what he thought at the time.

Nash was lucky enough that the internet introduced him to the person who would become one of his best friends: Stas. Anastasia Karanikolaou was a social media star in her own right. Stas or Stassi, who had more than 1.4 million followers on Instagram, lived in Calabasas, California, with Kylie Jenner and a couple of other people when Nash got to know her.

AT A MEETUP IN SANTA MONICA

I shot a video for my YouTube channel of her giving me a haircut, and my fans just loved her. But that was much later.

When Nash first came out to L.A. for the Grammys, Stas was kind enough to show him around. "These are the places you should go when you want to hang out," she instructed. "If you need to get away from all of the attention you can go to this beach, or you can go here. . . ." Serious insider stuff. Getting taken around the city by a native, who at the same time shared a similar point of view with Nash's, was priceless. Plus, she had a car. You can't get around L.A. without one.

Although I would. But again, that's later.

As soon as Nash came out to L.A. permanently, Stas was back on the case, updating him on all the cool places, introducing him to everybody, and making sure everything was smooth-flowing and normal. At least as normal as it could be. Whenever you go somewhere new, you need some kind of structure in which to meet new people—and Stas was Nash's structure.

Hanging out with Stas and all her friends felt right and normal, because in a way it wasn't that different than what Nash would have been doing in North Carolina. If he still lived at home, he would still be going out and having laughs with some cool people.

Of course, going to a *Teen Vogue* party or the VIP section of a club wasn't riding inner tubes on Lake Norman or sitting in the stands at his brother Will's football game. This was Hollywood, where he had some of the craziest damn nights of his life.

The scale of L.A., and the freedom that came with that, was just enormous when compared with Nash's hometown. He could see how a kid could get really lost or in real trouble here if he didn't have a center.

Going around with Stas, seeing the city at night, all those lights, there were so many things that were just mind-blowing. The most mind-blowing place of all was hands down the secret club that I basically hung out at every single night for six months.

The club that had no name was like something out of a movie, starting with its location: a private house on top of the Hollywood Hills, which some production company had bought. The actual club wasn't in the large house but behind it. So even if people somehow found out about the house, they still had to know the secret part of the property where the club was located—*past* the house and through an outside back patio where there were some stairs. Down the stairs, down and down, people went until they were in a room that was below ground level, like a bunker.

There were windows underground that looked directly into a pool that was on the property. (So if you were swimming in the pool, you could dive below the water and look into the club through the circular windows.) The club itself, lined with mirrors and couches, had a pool table and a big music setup.

VIEWING PARTY FOR
ENTOURAGE (THE
MOVIE) IN MARK
WAHLBERG'S BASEMENT

SNOWBOARDING IN BIG BEAR, CALIFORNIA

It was just as crazy as it sounds.

But the real reason it was a party every single night had to do with who was invited. The guest list was filled with people on a mission to have "fun." Other than that, the place was a real melting pot. Nash met so many different types of folks there—people not just from all over the world but who also did all different kinds of work. Naturally, there were the models, actors, and musicians. But there were also people doing cloud computing, digital animation, and app design. There were some who just painted. Others dreamed of writing and directing.

Although most of the kids he met at the club didn't have nearly the amount of stability that Nash had around him in terms of family and structure, they were all there pursuing their dreams. When Nash moved to L.A. he thought he was all alone, but seeing these kids who didn't have their lives figured out yet either made him feel less alone. They were in similar positions in that they wanted to entertain and had achieved a few opportunities to do so, but beyond that, it was up to focus and drive.

The anonymity of the club was its secret sauce. It was a place to have fun without worrying about people trying to take a picture or anything like that. Of course, it couldn't last. As soon as word got out, everyone wanted to go and experience this amazing underground bunker bar, and it got really crazy. Once that happened, there could easily be five hundred people lined up outside the gigantic gate that led into the property.

Nash was not unlike a lot of people he met in L.A. in that he had experienced instant fame and power, and now was trying to figure out what to do with it. Practically overnight he went from a lacrosse-playing high school kid in North Carolina to a top slot on the entertainment industry food chain, because of his social media followers.

Nash was dealing with adult things, and so let off steam in an adult way. A workaholic, he would wake up after six hours of sleep and immediately get to set or be producing content. Nash worked most days for twelve hours straight, and to blow off steam, he'd go out and get hammered. Sleep. Work. Get hammered. Repeat.

> Getting hammered was a mechanism to cope with the fact that I was working nonstop. Not that it was a great one. Looking back on it now, I had a drinking problem. But I didn't realize it at the time, because everyone around me was doing the same thing. Everyone went out every night, so it felt like the right thing to do.

Nash was very lost. He didn't know who or what to believe. Nothing seemed real, including the hype around him.

> I don't like people talking me up. To me, there's nothing worse than when someone makes a big deal out of something that shouldn't be that big a deal. Yeah, I have millions of followers online, but I didn't cure cancer. Despite the persona I sometimes

give off in my videos, in real life I'm very laid-back and keep to myself. I don't like to talk unless I have to talk. My goal is always to say less and listen more. But that's not the typical attitude in Hollywood, which is filled with self-promoters and fast talkers.

The entertainment industry is all about ranking people. There are levels and sublevels and sub-sublevels. Nash got a major education as soon as he arrived in Hollywood, as to who owns what and who runs what; where the money is; and the most popular crowd. He got all angles of the industry, as he was thrown into the scene, but ultimately, he saw things from the perspective of a normal guy—Nash's perspective.

In Hollywood the relationships and connections you make seem to be just as important as anything else you're doing. But Nash was uncomfortable with the whole "I worked with this person" or "I did this thing with that guy," which just seemed like a fancy version of name-dropping. He didn't want to live off relationships or connections, because the kind of people who do that . . . well, they suck. Whenever someone bragged about their eighteenth credit on some straight-to-video film, Nash wanted to scream, "Tell me who *you* are, not your credits."

Sifting through lame relationships isn't just something people do at parties in L.A. It's also a big part of the business. When Nash first arrived in town, he sat in meetings with the biggest talent agencies in the world. He got an earful of what they thought he wanted to hear. Nash met with all the major players in the business, and each and every one of them was the same. It's an agency's job to tell you what they think you want to hear. But until you actually get a contract on paper and read it, you have no idea what they are really going to do for you.

In my experience, listening to what's said in a meeting and reading a contract after the fact is so different, you will trip.

So many people in Hollywood get taken advantage of—Nash included. But in his case, things could have gone way worse than they actually went.

Yeah, I was only screwed in the very beginning of my career or in little places here and there. Basically the cost of doing business in Hollywood.

It took a while for Nash to learn how to separate fake from real out in L.A. Read someone's face? Use psychology? How could Nash know if people were working for him not against him?

It also took a while for him to learn how to adapt to L.A.— more specifically to fame, and the whole lifestyle that came with it.

I'm not saying, "Poor me, look how much it sucks to get paid to make cool videos," or anything like that. I knew that I was incredibly lucky for the opportunity to pursue my dream. But there's good and bad with everything.

MY FIRST COMIC-CON IN 2014

With every great success come haters. And the more success, the more haters. Taylor Swift, Justin Bieber, Jay-Z—all of them have experienced it. If you look at every giant in the entertainment industry, even the deceased, like Michael Jackson and Elvis, they have haters.

The one guy I can't understand having haters is Kurt Cobain. His songs gave voice to the mood of a whole generation. Why would someone hate on him for that? But he's got them, too.

On the internet, this stuff is even worse. There's a riot of haters online. They come in all forms. Some are softer than others, and those Nash usually just ignores.

If you want to drop comments after one of my videos that you hate my hair or think I'm an idiot, go ahead. I believe in alternative perspectives.

Those are the haters that just come with the territory. But there are others. . . .

The worst haters are the hackers. Nash was hacked a few times. They happened pretty much the same way, and they were all awful. After getting through the firewall, the hackers dove right into all his devices and those used by his family. There they found his address, everyone's Social Security numbers, etc. Once you're hacked you're hacked. You can't get your private information back, ever. It's more than annoying; it can be an imminent disaster. Personal information can be used to wreak all sorts of havoc.

The first time Nash was hacked, they found his family's address in North Carolina and decided to call the cops with a phony report of an emergency. "There's a bomb in the basement," they said. "A young white male with an M16 is holding his family hostage."

Nash was in New York at the time, but his dad, who had opened the front door to walk the dog around eleven thirty at night, was met with guns, dogs, and police officers.

"Get on the ground!" an officer screamed.

Chad was understandably totally confused, surprised, and terrified as he was thrown to the ground facedown and cuffed behind his back.

"How do we get to the basement?" the officer yelled.

"We don't have a basement," Nash's dad said, because he doesn't have a basement.

Eventually (a few hours later) the authorities figured out that it was a hack and fake call-in. But not before they raided the house and terrified everyone inside. Thank God it didn't happen at Nash's mom's house, because then Skylynn would have been subjected to that kind of nightmare—

and I would have a lot of trouble forgiving myself if I caused her such trauma.

That wasn't the last time hackers pranked the police into storming a Grier household. The next time it happened was at Nash's apartment in L.A., where he was sitting on the roof with Cam.

The roof was one of my favorite spots to just sit and think about life, because it was so calming up there.

On this particular night, Nash was eating tangerines. When he was done, he picked up the peels and started to climb down the ladder to get back into the building. Just then a helicopter went *swoosh* above his head.

Helicopters above Hollywood Boulevard are not out of the norm.

There's basically one flying around every ten seconds. All you ever hear are helicopters, which is part of what makes it so hard to shoot movies in Hollywood.

Still, this helicopter seemed to fly way too close overhead. Nash had never seen one come so close.

He kept going down the ladder and making his way back to his apartment. He had to hop over one side of the railing. That's when he looked up and saw that the helicopter really seemed to be hovering over his building.

It was so cool to watch that big lumbering flying machine just hanging there in midair that I didn't ask myself why it was doing that.

Then, thinking nothing more of it, he went back inside.

Nash figured they were looking for someone in the area, maybe using a high-powered scope or some other cool device. Whatever. They definitely weren't looking for him, a Vine star, right?

He walked downstairs and went into his room. After going to the bathroom, he lay down on his bed and started to play FIFA. But there was something really loud coming from outside the apartment building. He didn't put two and two together, but the helicopter had flown down the side of the building so that it was level with his window.

His curtains were drawn, but the noise was so deafening he put down his game and opened them to see what was making that racket. That's when he saw three snipers in the helicopter, pointed their guns right at him through his window!

Was I tripping? There was no way this was happening! What was happening?

Scared out of his mind, he fell back, onto the floor of his room, releasing the curtains.

"Whoa, whoa, whoa."

Did I actually have guns pointed at me? Did I just see that?

Nash didn't have time to question the soundness of his mind, because a second later, he heard a bunch of loud thuds on his ceiling. The snipers were on the top floor, and they had dropped like ten people onto the roof of his apartment. Soon those same people were busting open his back door.

Nash ran out of his room and toward the back door, where he came face-to-face with six fully armored men, screaming, "Put your hands up!"

Now he knew how his dad had felt. Not great.

Two innocent friends of his who happened to be over got the full treatment. The police handcuffed all of them behind their backs like they were in an episode of *Cops*.

It was scary as hell from the minute I saw that helicopter outside my window. You never just look out your window and happen to see people with guns in helicopters. It was like some scene out of a movie. Then to have all these badass cops interrogating me and my friends while were handcuffed, I thought I was going to piss my pants. I was lucky I had just gone to the bathroom.

As soon as Nash could get his vocal cords to make a noise, he informed the cops of what he suspected to be the source of the misunderstanding. "By the way, I don't know what's going on," he said. "I don't know what we did. But this is probably a prank, guys. You need to make sure that it's not, before you do this to anyone else."

They weren't convinced. They spent a few hours questioning everyone, trying to identify them and get to the bottom of who called in the terrorist threat coming from Nash's apartment.

They never told Nash what the call had been or what was so bad they needed to drop a bunch of commandos down from a helicopter to storm his place. The whole experience wasn't just scary. It was humiliating. Nash felt awful the entire time, for himself and his friends. Even after the police left the apartment, everyone else in the building was standing outside trying to find out what was going on. They wanted to see the train wreck, which turned out to be Nash and his group.

That goes to show you how crazy a hater can be and how extreme his or her actions can go.

Nash ended up getting kicked out of that apartment—but not because of the *Apocalypse Now*–style helicopter scene. Nine months after the swat team stormed his apartment, Nash and his roommates were kindly told they were not welcome. It was for a bunch of other stuff too, but out of all the people who came and went in that first place he lived in L.A., Nash had one room-mate who was particularly troublesome. The guy would throw water balloons out of the window and stuff like that. So when it came time to renew their lease, the building management sent them a letter of about fifty things they did that were not okay. They ranged from speeding in the parking garage to general noise complaints.

I didn't even have a car, so the garage drag racing couldn't have been me. As to the other grievances, I don't know. Maybe two or three of them were me. But most of them weren't me. Really.

CHAPTER 8

Hackers aren't the only haters out there. Nash also had to learn how to deal with misrepresentations of him in the media.

In the summer of 2014, not long after Nash had moved to L.A., he experienced an episode of social media backlash that stemmed from a Vine posted two years prior.

At the time of this Vine, Nash was a fourteen-year-old kid in North Carolina who had just downloaded his profile on the app and was using the medium as a way to get his friends at school to laugh.

I wish I didn't have to repeat the content of the video I made, because I'm deeply ashamed that I ever thought something like that was anything close to funny. But if you didn't read about my video controversy online, then you won't understand the

*rest of this chapter unless I describe it. So here
it is:*

Nash took a TV commercial for a home oral HIV test and screamed the word *fag* over it.

*There it is. It was derogatory and entirely
offensive—I never imagined how many people I would
hurt by making it. It was a dumb attempt to get
a laugh from my peers, and there is no excuse for it.*

Online, Nash received a very different kind of feedback than the juvenile laughter he'd gotten at Davidson Day. He had about twelve hundred followers around that time, so he wasn't used to getting any comments on his posts. Again, his Vines were more about reactions from kids at his school. If there were ever any comments, Nash hardly read them. But on this one, which didn't have many likes or re-Vines (understandably so), the comments were brewing, so he took time to read through them. It was a real education for Nash.

"This is super-offensive."

"You can't do this here."

"Ever heard of human equality?"

"You're shaming a whole group of people!"

It might sound naïve, but at the time, Nash was completely caught off guard. In his small corner of the world, he hadn't known anyone who was openly gay. That's why the kids in his school laughed at his joke, which was anything but funny. They laughed to feel more comfortable about things they didn't understand.

I absolutely see that now. But at the time, I had no clue how hurtful and cruel my video was. I just thought, This will be popular.

The followers who commented gave him real insight into how he was negatively affecting other people. Nash seriously reflected on these comments and realized that his cheap attempt at a joke was wrong. So he deleted the entire post.

However, as they say, you can't really delete anything from the internet (which is why it's a good idea not to put anything on social media you don't want future employers, friends, girlfriends, or boyfriends to know about). Fast-forward two years later, and Nash is living in L.A. Someone got ahold of the video and re-uploaded it to the internet.

YouTuber and LGBT activist Tyler Oakley shared the video on Twitter, where he had two million followers, stating, "Call me and people like me 'fag' all you want, but spreading false information about deadly diseases is next level."

Tyler's tweets set off an immediate firestorm, as TMZ and many other online outlets picked up the story. The media had a field day. Nash tried to read as many articles as he could, but the more he read, the angrier he got. His anger wasn't because the articles were reporting on what a jerk he had been.

I had been a jerk.

No, it was because for the most part the articles made it seem as if he had posted this video recently, when in fact he had posted it years earlier and deleted it shortly thereafter.

Although the articles made me look small-minded, mean-spirited, and, frankly, evil, my story put the spotlight on a bigger social issue surrounding homophobia.

When he was enlightened by those who challenged him to change his perspective, that's exactly what he did. Moving out to L.A.—a place where there are all kinds of people living all kinds of lifestyles—only furthered his social-emotional education and opened his mind.

Why shouldn't you be able to love whomever you love?

Nash reacted honestly to and learned from his mistake, because people were willing to say "Hey! Stand over here and see what it's like."

After that Vine was reposted, everyone jumped on the anti-Nash bandwagon, including a bunch of people whom he'd never met, interacted with, or had anything to do with.

The reactions from the public were all shades of angry. His public apology for his past actions was considered insincere and nothing more than a publicity ploy.

But I was, and still am, deeply sorry.

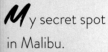
*M*y secret spot in Malibu.

*M*y favorite spot in Malibu.

Looking for cliff-jumping spots in Bali in 2017. "You jump, you die," a fisherman told me.

First snow of 2019.

Encounter with a wild giraffe in South Africa.

At the Australia tour's photo shoot with my manager/ attorney Melinda and Hayes.

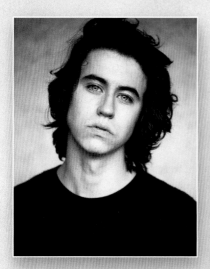

*H*eadshot from my first fashion week in Paris.

*C*hecking out the skyline in Dubai.

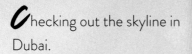

A school in Swaziland celebrating getting clean water.

*D*ubai desert summer. It was 130 degrees!

*O*n the French Polynesian island of Mooréa.

*S*ometimes it takes someone else to find yourself. (Swaziland)

*M*ooréa's Coco Beach (I recycled the water bottle).

*4*lways a great day to
be a Mountaineer.

*E*xploring waterfalls in
West Virginia.

*T*he view from outside Dubai.

*D*oing what I love with who I love.

*C*ape Town sunrise from the top of Lion's Head.

Nash needed to make sure people knew that this was a messed-up thing he said as a kid. He wanted people to know him for who he really was, an openhearted human willing to learn. But how do you do that? He had already publicly apologized, and it wasn't making a difference. That kind of thing doesn't fit in a tweet. He had to go long format.

Nash decided to write something for the *Huffington Post*, because he had had a positive experience with that online media outlet in the past. Nash asked if he could write about the incident, and the editors gave him the go-ahead. He figured it would at least be a chance for him to get a word in about what happened after everyone else had already weighed in.

Nash submitted a piece that attempted to explain the entire story of how he had made a terrible mistake when he was a kid. "I, Nash Grier, have made more mistakes than I can remember," he wrote.

This was his attempt at honest writing in his voice without publicists adding anything. He described the loneliness every teenager feels and the need to fit in. Then he went on to explain his version of how he did that—through Vine, making kids laugh. "As a kid from a private school, I was very sheltered from the real world," he wrote. "I didn't know the meaning behind what I was saying when I made the video. I didn't know the people I was hurting."

Nash also wrote about his subsequent public apologies and the sadness he felt when people thought the video was new—and that he was a "hate monger."

"If there is one thing I stand for in life, it is do whatever makes you happy. I have never and never will be against same-sex relationships or marriages. I can't stress to you enough how far off the title 'homophobic' is from my actual personality."

He called for the acceptance and respect of anyone, whether "black, white, gay, straight, Asian, bisexual, Australian, tall, fat." Happily, the article was generally met with love. LGBT organizations asked if Nash would become an advocate by doing campaigns. He did a few shoots, like for the NOH8 Campaign, an LGBT rights group that takes photos of celebrities with duct tape over their mouths and "NOH8" written on their cheeks as a way to raise awareness about discrimination and its effects. Although NOH8 founder Jeff Parshley was willing to forgive Nash, not everyone was. Some social media stars and their followers thought it was hypocritical of Nash to promote a positive LGBT message—as if it is impossible to be truly, genuinely sorry.

Whatever my detractors said, personally, it was pretty cool to see the world rise up against hateful ignorance and stop it in its tracks. It was definitely a transformative experience for me. Anytime mistakes are made, opportunities to learn are created. So, in some weird way, it felt nice knowing other ignorant people would learn what not to do from me.

Finally, Nash's hateful Vine video controversy died. Except it didn't.

In January 2016, Nash tweeted for his fans to share their favorite videos of his. The actress Ariel Winter—who had never met Nash—reignited the whole controversy by reminding her followers of the offensive Vine from years prior.

Unfortunately, it swept through the internet *again*. And, *again*, a lot of people thought that this was a new Vine and a belief of Nash's.

Nash struggled with how to react. Should he address it? That would only be adding fuel to the fire of something he felt he had already dealt with. At this point, anyone who followed him knew what he promoted, what he preached, and what he pushed. They would also know that he doesn't promote anything that isn't true to his heart.

Nash was in a tough position. He didn't want to respond publicly because he understood that it would only draw more attention to it. But, Winter's original post had already started a war on Twitter between the people who accepted Nash had changed and grown as a person, and those who didn't. Winter wrote, "You only apologized for that video and stopped using that phrase after it started affecting your pocketbook and chipping away at your fame. So, no, I don't believe your views have changed. I just believe your forum for spouting them has changed."

Nash responded to Winter by messaging her directly: "Would

LOVE to talk to you & explain why your opinion about others' opinions are far from reality."

Her response was, "lol I'm good 😒"

No matter how much you disagree with someone else, you should still be willing to have a dialogue, Nash reasoned. And that was the end of the conversation for Nash.

It was painful to sit by while the controversy continued to gain momentum not only online but also on mainstream television, like when Winter denounced Nash during an appearance on *The Talk*. As he watched her describe this awful Nash Grier guy, he was practically shouting at the screen, "Damn! I'm on your side! I'm on the right side!" The discussion was just one side of the story.

It reminded him of the *Huffington Post*'s coverage of his "feud" with Winter posted a week earlier on the site. Nash was shocked when he read the last line of the article: "We wish more celebrities would use their platform to call out racism, homophobia and sexism," the article said. "Keep on killing it, Ariel."

Wow. The same organization that agreed to publish his full apologetic account of the homophobic Vine also chose to disregard everything he had shared within it as truth on its site.

All right. I get it.
This is the media.
Another learning experience.

Nash had to recognize that because he was in the public eye there will always be some element of unwanted media attention in his life. Having people who don't know the first thing about him writing misleading content is just part of this business. At the end of the day, however rightly or wrongly he was perceived, Nash still knew who he really was and he told himself, "I have to be okay with that."

NASH'S
FAVORITE GUILTY PLEASURE

Sitting on my ass all day and watching things—
movies, shows, videos, etc. The only part I feel
guilty about is how much sitting I do.

CHAPTER 9

By the time Nash was kicked out of his Hollywood apartment, he was ready to move on anyway. He had been depressed in that place, because he was experiencing what it meant to be alone for the first time in his life. Later, though, when he got acclimated to feeding himself and doing laundry, his disillusionment with the industry was growing. He was starting to lose sight of why he had moved all the way to California. He needed a change of scenery. *Definitely.*

So Nash moved to the Valley. If you're not familiar with L.A., that's the San Fernando Valley. Home to the original Valley girls, this suburban area filled with strip malls might not be the coolest part of the city. But because rents were a lot cheaper, Nash was able to get an awesome place.

He moved into a real house, a corner property with two bedrooms, two bathrooms, a big living room, fenced-in yard, tennis court, and pool.

I know, fancy.

The best part of that place wasn't the pool or the tennis court—but a studio. An amazing gem of a room, the studio looked like a library with wood paneling, bookshelves, and stairs that ran the height of the double-high ceilings. It was beautiful and might allow for the nicest creative vibes and energy.

He hoped this would be a place with enough room physically and metaphorically to figure out what he wanted to do with his life. The questions so many teens ask themselves swirled around in his head.

What am I most passionate about?

What am I best at?

What do I have the most potential to do?

What would be the most rewarding? The most fun?

He had a lot of thinking to do. Unfortunately the house in the Valley turned out *not* to be the spot in which to do it.

The secret club Nash and his crew used to hang at had been shut down. There was no formal closing; the secret party just faded away. For a while, the Janoskians took up the mantle. The Janoskians (which stands for Just Another Name of Silly Kids in Another Nation) is a YouTube comedy group out of Australia, where they are huge. Nash spent a lot of time with the three brothers and two friends who had moved to L.A. On the internet, they were known for their prank videos and mockumentaries. But in real life, they were known for throwing the biggest parties. The Gatsbys of Nash's set, they hosted a house party every Wednesday.

But all "good" things must come to an end and eventually they moved, or their house got shut down. Whatever it was, everyone was looking for that next spot.

When Nash moved to the Valley, it coincided with all his crew's regular parties getting shut down. Nash had a roommate, who saw a perfect solution to their social problems, or at least his. The roommate was one of Nash's good friends from North Carolina, who moved to L.A., and threw parties at Nash's house, especially when he wasn't home.

Nash traveled a lot. Still does.

I'm probably on the road more than I'm home. When I'm not on the road, I'm home pretty much 100 percent of the time. So I need to have a place I can leave and come back to and know it will be just as I left it— calm and not filled with strangers.

He hated leaving the house in the Valley, because he'd come back either to a party going on or the aftermath of one. The messes were just awful. The house always seemed to be getting trashed, and they were racking up the noise complaints.

His address got out really fast, way too fast. There were always too many people there. Inevitably someone Nash didn't know got his phone out and started taking pictures of his house or the people in it. That was not okay. That's what started happening in the Valley, and it didn't feel good. When fans actually broke into his house a couple of times, Nash shut down the party house ASAP.

Every day there was a fat-ass party at my house. There was not a day when there were less than ten people in that house. And the party wasn't even contained inside. Sometimes it got to block-party proportions. One time, it seemed like every member of every USC sorority showed up at my house. That was a very crazy time.

When Nash and the other original MagCon guys first moved out to L.A., the party scene was big *and* relentless. It makes sense: guys like Nash, Shawn Mendes, Jack & Jack, and Cam were coming from much smaller places and totally enthralled with everything this new city had to offer. The friends Nash made were all over the place—from Johanna, his videographer, to guys as random as his driver. They were all different ages and all different types, which was great. If he were still living in North Carolina, everyone he hung out with would be just like him.

Nash was looking for a surrogate family in his friends, and the Valley was home base. But he was tired of partying. He was sick of drinking and would rather play pickup games of soccer on the tennis court. His disillusionment with L.A. encompassed his entire life—from getting hammered, to the blowback he received in the media, to the scripts that didn't seem to be going anywhere.

When Nash first arrived in Hollywood, a lot of people pigeonholed him as someone who was only good on Vine. He kept on pushing the idea that he could do so much more—but he worried that people who didn't believe in him were determining every aspect of his career. They got him projects, negotiated them, scheduled and filled his days. It was "Do this; do this; do this." Take this acting class. Go on this audition.

I was basically paying people to boss me around.

Nash needed to rethink not only *how* he worked but with whom he was working.

He was in a bad place in terms of how he felt about the direction of his work. He wasn't inspired, but worse than that, he knew he was one mess-up away from being owned or disowned.

The situation was not good at all. I had to take control, and that first started with reflecting on what was really important and meaningful to me.

The essence of what Nash came out to L.A. to do can be traced back to when he was seven years old. Once the custody schedule became more flexible, Chad would take his sons to a restaurant called Prime Time every Tuesday—because every Tuesday kids ate for free. The Grier boys would go crazy on the homemade southern buffet of pulled pork, meat loaf, okra, mashed potatoes, and anything else that was delicious *and* could give you a heart attack. But hands down, the best part of the meal was the ice cream machine, which, like everything else in the buffet, was unlimited.

One part of their Tuesday-night ritual was an ice cream contest. Every time they went, their dad would challenge his sons to see who could finish an ice cream cone, top to bottom, fastest. Even though his dad could eat an ice cream cone in what seemed like one bite, Nash had it in his head that he could beat him. Once, he actually did beat him. He just basically swallowed an entire ice cream cone. It was awful. It hurt. It did not feel good physically. But it felt great to win. Even better, though, was the reaction from the crowd. The entire restaurant was dying laughing, or at least it felt like that.

I remember that feeling as a kid, and I remember having the exact same feeling ten years later. It didn't matter if it was at Prime Time or on a soundstage. I wanted to do something as simple as make someone laugh. Overall, that's what I wanted to do with my life. I believed that making people laugh in real life was just as important as doing it on camera.

Although it's an artificial re-creation, the entertainment industry needs to be grounded in true moments like the ice-cream contest if it's any kind of real and meaningful entertainment.

Nash got his start in the business by blending reality and entertainment. The videos that brought him all that early attention were public pranks with cameras filming him—like jumping into a fountain in the middle of the mall.

He loved making his Vines and knew he wanted to make people laugh. But he didn't know what the ultimate goal was. What was going to keep him going for the next ten years? His funny prank and interview-style videos were unsustainable. As good as they are, it was hard to imagine making those kind of videos deep into the future.

Even while he was still in North Carolina, he had already started to experiment with scripted material. Nash had skits on his YouTube channel where he played different characters. He took his inspiration from watching others, like masters of the genre Keegan-Michael Key and Jordan Peele. Their Comedy Central sketch show, *Key & Peele,* of which he watched every single episode from its five seasons, helped shape his creative taste.

Knowing what you like and making what you like are two different things entirely. By the time Nash had moved to L.A., he was making full-on little movies for the 4.5 million subscribers to his YouTube channel, while continuing to make content for all his various other platforms. He had gained nearly 5 million Twitter followers and more than 8 million on Instagram.

Almost overnight, he went from having to conceive, direct, shoot, and star in his own videos to working with a production staff to tell his stories. The basic challenges of any narrative still rested on his shoulders. He needed to write compelling scenes and characters, interacting in such a way as to tell a bigger story than the actual words on the page.

In the beginning, Nash was definitely the hot new thing in Hollywood. Everyone wanted to get a piece of his platform and followers. He went and pitched projects to some of the biggest producers out there, who immediately were ready to turn them into studio movies. It was a funny thing, because on the one hand he did think he had done a relatively good job creating a plot and characters, and having big-name companies validate his ideas with offers gave him a sense of accomplishment. On the other hand, Nash was also perplexed. He walked out of more than one meeting, thinking, *What is going on? What just happened?*

Nash said a couple of paragraphs in a boardroom, and that's all that was needed to call the next day with a complete budget for a feature-length film? How did those guys make that leap when they didn't know what the scenes were or how long the movie would take or what it would look like? Why was there suddenly a price tag on it?

> Even now, after I've gotten used to it, I still hate the fact that money comes first—and only later creativity and passion. It should be the other way around.

Everything on his plate was put there by someone else—and it was all pretty much for money.

Nash didn't completely agree with his former team on their plans for him. At the time, they were trying not only to get him experience doing different kinds of projects but also to bring some stability to his career.

The film *The Outfield* was definitely part of that early career-building period of his life. Nash was psyched when the deal came together for Cam and him to star in his first film! Although Cam had already been in *Expelled, The Outfield*—about three baseball players and best friends figuring out their real passion in life during the tumultuous time that is senior year of high school—was Nash's acting debut. Written by Lydia Genner and developed and codirected by Eli Gonda and Michael Goldfine, *The Outfield* also starred Joey Bragg, who does stand-up but is best known for his role on the Disney Channel's *Liv and Maddie*. It also featured Olivia Stuck as Cam's love interest and the talented actress Caroline Sunshine as Emily, the strong-willed, protective girlfriend of Nash's character, Jack.

The movie was a huge challenge for him. Although he had taken hours and hours of acting classes, this was the real thing. And while he wanted to keep up his internet content, he also was interested in transitioning to film. As they say, you never get a second chance at a first impression.

The team behind the camera created the character of Jack in part from Nash's life. The writers and producers wanted to draw inspiration from reality—not just Nash's but their own as well. They met a lot to discuss the script, so that by the time filming began, the whole project felt serious and real. It also felt important to Nash, because the theme of the movie—how you need to come to terms with who you really are and not just what everybody wants you to be—had become something he was grappling with in real life.

When it comes to acting, no matter how many classes you take or how many acting coaches you have, it's not something that you can understand before you do it. When you try to act—and so many people do—that's when you mess up. The two months he spent filming *The Outfield* were an amazing experience for Nash. Getting to be another person for a while is a real gift. In playing Jack, Nash got to return to sports, be on the field again. Even spending time in a "classroom" was sort of nice.

When I reflect on my performance, however, I realize I didn't know what acting actually was. Acting is not trying to do anything; it's being. It's living. It's being as normal as possible. That is the truth. The most truthful people are the best actors. Acting is reacting. You put yourself in the position, the ultimate context, and then anything you do or say simply adds to the scenario.

It isn't easy to be natural, authentic, or honest on a film set where there's a whole department for lighting and sound. There's a whole department for Camera One! On *The Outfield* there were codirectors, a gaffer, hair, and makeup. At any given location, there were easily 150 people working to create the image. It felt more like an army than a group of artists.

Everything is happening in the moment and needs to be a truthful, real experience. And the cameras are just there to capture it. While filming, people, Nash included, think too much about the filming. The best movie actors don't worry about where anything is, other than their head. What's the mind-set of their character in the moment—you just walked in on your wife cheating on you or your best friend killed himself. That's the only thing that should exist. You feel it; it happens. You do it. It's real. You become the person.

That's the genius behind Leonardo DiCaprio. He becomes Howard Hughes or Jordan Belfort. After learning everything he possibly can about his characters, he just becomes them.

The Outfield ended up being an international commercial success, becoming the bestselling drama on iTunes when it was released—even outselling *Jurassic World*. But for Nash personally, more than a year had passed since he signed the deal to make *The Outfield*, and then another year went by between shooting and its release. He had changed so much in that period. He still had more that he wanted to achieve, particularly when it came to his artistic vision.

In terms of performing, Nash loved getting a reaction out of people and having fun. But he didn't have a clue about the depth of the craft.

A lot of people don't. The best actors understand what it is, because they either are born with natural talent or develop it through passion and grit. I have an inherent ability to joke, become other people, shape-shift, and relay messages.

The Outfield inspired Nash to want to be better. He didn't want to be typecast. Every time he stepped on set, he felt another part of him learning and developing. Although he had a long road ahead of him, he knew the right steps he needed to take to get where he wanted to be—not only as an actor but also as a writer, director, and filmmaker.

After Nash moved to the Valley, he began his own private graduate course in the history of film. He studied every movie, short film, and interview with an actor or director.

On WatchMojo, I checked out the top 10 of everything—the top 10 movie trailers, the top 10 improv scenes, the top 10 Method actors. Everything I watched, even bad movies, made me better. I watched every Oscar-winning film there is, ever. I went on a _Godfather_ marathon, watching all three straight through. I went as far back as silent films, watching important classics like _Metropolis_. As I progressed into the 1930s and beyond, I marveled at how quickly the storytelling of motion pictures evolved, from a black-and-white screen with no sound and flares, to movies with sound and sound effects, to movies with color, and beyond. Although we're now in the limitlessness of the digital era, moving images are fairly new in the grand scheme of things.

Nash fell in love with master creators, people like Alfred Hitchcock, Martin Scorsese, Quentin Tarantino, and Stanley Kubrick. With all the choices that need to be made in any movie (every scene can go in ten completely different ways, and it's up to the director to guide the action and feel), these geniuses put all the different elements together to tell complete stories. They question all formulas of whatever genre they're working in. From the body language of the characters, to the camera shots, to the music, their movies give life to the most interesting visions.

So it wasn't just acting Nash needed to study but visual effects, animation, voice-over, sound mixing, and editing, too. He listened to soundtracks in movies by Oscar winners like John Williams, as well as straight-up sound effects. He also took an interest in the financial and business side of the industry. For example, he researched the highest-grossing films and the biggest money losers. Whenever he stayed in a hotel, one of the first things he did when he got into his room was check out which studios they had deals with to offer movies on their TVs. Everything was a learning opportunity.

I'm a trailer junkie. I like to see how movies are promoted, what's popping and what's not. I watch everything with a very different perspective than the average consumer. It's all part of this big study of mine. If there's a bad commercial, and I can see why it was a bad commercial, that's good information.

Whether it was learning how to use current editing programs, like Final Cut or Premiere, or software for producing music and making beats, like Logic and Pro Tools, or discovering media deals made with hotel chains, Nash put himself through a self-taught film-school experience.

The year he spent in the Valley, which allowed him at least a little more space and time to think, Nash experimented with so much. His goal was to be as open and real as he could. He painted, studied music, got into producing, and wrote in his journal all the time. He spent hours sitting in front of a computer, canvas, or notebook, challenging himself to push life to the limits. "Go ahead," he told himself. "You're seventeen years old and you've got life by the balls. Write out what you want to do and don't mess up."

Through that long process of reflection, he figured out what he wanted to do, what he was truly passionate about: he wanted to tell stories.

I want to affect people. I want to evoke emotion and spread knowledge.

His Vines and YouTube videos created a powerful connection between a huge number of people and him. It made him happy to make them happy.

If I can just see someone walk away at a meet and greet with a big smile, then I'm gratified, too.

The internet is that place where you have the freedom to do almost anything you want. Going out and creating his own opportunities was where Nash felt most at home. How many times had he done something no one thought he had the capability to do, only to have it take him a step in another direction? He made inroads into all different kinds of industries by just trying things out.

I hope I never stop doing any of that. At the same time, I want to produce material with

longevity. I want to create messages that will live forever. I want to tell stories with deep meanings, whether they are about rapid eye movement or the depiction of Native Americans in film. I want to help shape culture and society—for the better.

Ten, twenty, thirty years from now, I still want to be telling stories that are relevant and timeless. I want to make the most intricate, well-constructed movies with layers upon layers of discovery for the audience. Basically, I want to bring emotions out of people, and to tell the best stories. That is what keeps me moving forward. That is what I love to do.

NASH'S

FAVORITE COMFORT FOODS

- Potatoes

- Collard greens

- Boiled peanuts

CHAPTER 10

We were all put on this earth to love. I think as
humans, that's ultimately our main purpose: to love.

I believe everyone has this loving nature within,
but it often fades as we grow. Early in our lives is
when love is most natural and most evident. You can
see it so clearly with babies, who are just curious
creatures absorbing love. There is no better example
than a mother holding her child right after birth.
That has to happen for all kinds of reasons, physical,
emotional, and many others we can't even put into
words. Reasons that are above us.

I believe in a God, a higher power that created
the universe, earth, and all the beautiful intricacies
and mysteries of life.

Nash didn't always think like that. He didn't always put women on a pedestal. Like a lot of little boys, he used to think girls had cooties.

I remember the first time I ever thought girls <u>did</u> <u>not</u> have cooties. I was eight years old and watching an episode of <u>Full House</u>. Yes, Mary-Kate and Ashley Olsen were officially my first crushes. Watching them on TV was a revelation, because it was the very first moment that I felt something other than revulsion toward a member of the opposite sex. (After that, I watched everything the Olsens did—their specials, movies, it didn't matter how girly.)

Nash's first interest in a real girl—

the Olsens are real people, but a girl I could actually see in real life and not just on a screen—

was Hannah. They had grown up in the same neighborhood, and her family was good friends with his. But in fourth grade, they started to hang out, just the two of them. She was a gymnast, and their relationship consisted of stuff like kicking each other in the shins.

That's how you know you like each other when you are in fourth grade.

It wasn't until seventh grade that Nash had a real relationship. Well, real at least for a seventh grader. It was real to the point that they would actually go on dates where they talked to each other.

But that was about it. This was an *older* woman. She was in eighth grade, and one of the prettiest girls in middle school. Nash took a lot of heat for even trying to go out with her. It wasn't easy winning her over.

> To be honest, I don't know how I did it. Maybe, even though I was only thirteen, I was just smooth with words. I used to send her the longest texts from my flip phone. I spent so much time clicking through the letters (4, 4, 4, 5, 5, 5, 9, 9, 9) until I had composed my ode to her.

It worked, because even though she was way out of his league, they wound up dating for a year.

But like lots of love stories, Nash wound up getting his heart broken.

> I'm not saying we were in love or anything. We had this weird relationship that we thought was normal, because we were in middle school and didn't know any better. No one has a relationship-relationship in middle school. Still, we were definitely together, and then one day—just like that—we weren't.

Maybe when she started ninth grade she didn't want to be a high schooler going out with an eighth grader. Who could blame her? That's kind of weird.

> All I know is, suddenly she was with another guy.

That was just the start of Nash's problems with women. Believe it or not, this mega social media star had a lot of awful experiences with girls, ranging from being ignored to being stood up.

Nash never had trouble finding a girl to go to a school dance with him or anything like that.

I'm good at charming my way into situations, and girls will go for that for an afternoon or night.

But as he continued to grow and mature, he wanted to really connect with someone else, find the kind of person he could talk to for an entire day and learn things from. But that didn't come easily.

Back in North Carolina, Nash was always having to change schools, which made it hard to have a real friendship with girls his age, which is the start to any meaningful relationship, no matter how old you are. Nash never seemed to have enough time to get to know them or have them get to know him. His core group—the guys on the lacrosse team, his brother Will, and his best friends—were mostly older than him. The girls they hung around with didn't want anything to do with Nash, at least not romantically. So on a basic level, he didn't know *how* to meet girls.

And as a fourteen-year-old, it felt a little early to be setting up an online dating profile.

After he became "Nash Grier the Vine Star"

(or whatever you want to call it),

it became a lot easier to meet girls.

That's an understatement—I met thousands of girls at events like MagCon and ten times that online. But that didn't make my relationships with them any easier.

The idea of having a girlfriend when Nash first moved to L.A. was unfathomable. It didn't even cross his mind. He could hardly deal with the idea of making new friends—or eating a healthy meal. Before he could deal with the attention of one person, he had to learn to deal with all the attention he was getting from lots of people. Having strangers ask him for pictures or autographs all the time was definitely not an easy thing to get used to. A lot of times he felt like an object.

I hated it.

It seemed like in every interaction he had, someone wanted something from him—each in his or her own way. There were businesspeople trying to take advantage of him with shady deals. There were paparazzi trying to make money off pictures of him coming out of his apartment or going into a party. There didn't seem to be anyone out there who was genuine.

You meet a lot of people in Hollywood who use that as a marketing tool, though: "I'm the one that's out here who's nice, or who's helpful!" And actually they are not.

Nash was so untrusting that he wound up keeping to himself a lot, at least emotionally.

In general, I tend to keep to myself—especially at parties. I'm not the guy who's going up to girls saying, "Yet's ha-cha-cha-cha!!" I'm the guy who's watching the guy going, "Yet's ha-cha-cha-cha!!" My favorite activity at a party (other than watching the party animal in his natural habitat) is to find a cool room where there are no other people and just sit there with my friends and talk.

He was in a funny place, being both closed and open at the same time. While professionally, he was exposing himself to anything and everything in an effort to educate himself, socially Nash was shut down. He did not want to let anyone get too close to him, for fear of getting used.

I was so bottled up and to-myself in the same period I was making some of the greatest connections ever. It was ironic and confusing.

When it came to girls, everything was magnified. There were a few who were interested in him, but not for the right reasons. He became like a psychology major, studying body language and reading in between the lines as he tried to get to the bottom of what they were really thinking or their ultimate goal in hanging out with him. What he discovered through his investigations was that most were looking for a relationship to gain publicity or popularity.

You shouldn't get in a relationship with someone because you like the way they are perceived by other people, or because you like their status. It shouldn't be for any other reason than "We're better together than we are when we're not together."

We is better than you and me.

Even though he'd never had a real romantic relationship, Nash knew what one was by looking at the example of other people who were actually in love, people like his mom and stepdad.

When Nash's mom, Elizabeth, started dating his stepdad, Johnnie, Nash knew he was into her. But he understood Johnnie really *loved* his mom by the way the man treated him and his brothers. Johnnie didn't have any children of his own when he met Nash's mom and could easily have been resentful of three annoying boys always around and needing stuff. Not Johnnie, though. He would go out of his way to do anything for Nash. He built a half-pipe for Nash, so he could do tricks on his bike. He woke up at 6 a.m. to drive Nash to football games or lacrosse tournaments. Johnnie spent hours and hours on him and his brothers, without complaint. In fact, he seemed happy to do it.

That's when I was like, "Damn! He must really love my mom!" Because to devote yourself to kids who aren't even yours, you must have a lot of love in your heart.

Of course, Johnnie and Elizabeth eventually had their own kid—a daughter, Skylynn. And Nash was there—in the room—when his mom gave birth to her. It was his mom's idea. At first, Nash was totally perplexed. "What? Why?" he asked.

"Because you're going to be the guy holding someone's hand one day," she said.

He didn't know what to think. Just twelve years old, being a dad seemed as far in the future as the sun burning up.

But, like I said before, my mom is a wise woman. She has a connection with the earth and a very good moral compass. She knows what's right and what's wrong; what's natural and not natural; what's supposed to happen and what's not.

Nash's mom has always been able to help him with things *before* they've happened.

You don't have to prepare for something if you're already prepared for it—and that's what Nash's mom has done for most of his childhood

(and continues to do).

Because of her, Nash feels like he's prepared for pretty much anything that's thrown his way.

Every experience, whether good or bad, widens the spectrum of existence—and that's what my mom gave me by inviting me to witness the birth of Skylynn.

Will and Hayes were also in the hospital when Skylynn was born. So was Elizabeth's twin sister (who wound up studying to become a doula—a person trained in assisting a woman during childbirth—maybe because she was so inspired by the experience). Nash played computer games while he waited for his mother to get in her delivery room. When she finally arrived, a bunch of stuff happened, then at last the doctor came in.

When the real action began, I don't remember what I was thinking, or what I was watching. The whole process, everything happening in that small room, took on a life of its own. But I was in there, right beside my mom.

The feeling Nash got from being a witness to a new life coming into this world was less like a realization and more like a hit in the chest. Like a hit in the chest from a lacrosse ball. Hard, powerful, and unforgettable. It was just a beautiful thing, because of its universality.

That's why his mom wanted him to be there. Although it's not typical for mothers to invite their sons to watch them give birth, Nash was grateful Elizabeth did. He was glad to be familiar with the process, because when he had kids one day he would be able to fully support his partner. The last thing a woman in labor, who has spent more than nine months preparing for this moment, wants is a squeamish man unprepared to give his all. In that moment, there are no do-overs, so you can't have any issues. You've got to be seamless. You've got to be ready to go.

My mom's training of me to be a good man didn't stop with Skylynn's birth. Being a big brother to a little sister has been invaluable in my appreciation of what it means to be a girl.

Nash loved his baby sister from day one. Not long after Skylynn was born, he could make her laugh.

If you look at the expression on a baby's face, you can see their thoughts, eyes, and body all working together in concert. They're either supercurious, or supermad, or supersad, or superhappy. Whatever the emotion, it's complete. Their spectrum of existence is so small because they've just getting started, so every little thing from getting your toes tickled to being hungry is so huge.

Being a big part of shaping Skylynn's range of experiences was so interesting and rewarding for Nash. Just doing the littlest thing had the biggest effect on her. He'd ask her, "What's Mom's coffee?" And she'd go, "Hot! Hot!" Or he'd say, "Do your mean face!" And she'd go, "Grrr." That might not seem like a big deal, but even doing a routine as small as that several times a week, making that little connection, helped create the person she was becoming.

WILD SKY

A VIDEO OF SKYLYNN FILMED FOUR YEARS TO THE DAY AFTER
I POSTED THE ORIGINAL VIDEO, "MEET MY SISTER"

For Nash, watching her grow up was amazing—and to document it was a big gift. Because he had so much footage of her, he could go back and watch how much she changed every year of her life.

It's a true gift to be able to go back to the mind-set I was in and the stage of development she was in, and think about how far we've both come. Watching the old videos of her (even stuff like me hitting her with a pillow while she laughs her butt off) only reinforces how much of a bond I've had with my sister.

Will, Hayes, and Nash have all influenced Skylynn's life a lot. Just like Nash learned so much about playing football from watching Will, Skylynn has absorbed everything her older brothers have to offer and taken it a step further. A quick learner, she's always aware of everything going on in her surroundings.

Skylynn is very sassy.

Skylynn also changed Nash. She's definitely made him gentler and opened his eyes to a lot of things.

It's easier to put a lot more in perspective when you have a little person right there looking up to you. It's impossible not to ask yourself, "What if I was a young person right now?"

Being with Skylynn made Nash contemplate so many questions about her and all kinds of children.

What is another kid the same age thinking in Asia right now?

What are the issues that surround her life?

What directly impacts her?

How can she save the world?

That little girl taught me a heck of a lot, including the fundamental truth that everyone in someone else's life helps to shape that life. When we engage with another person in a deep way, we alter their existence and at the same time are altered ourselves.

That profound way of looking at relationships made it really hard to trade in for the kind of shallow romances Nash saw all around him in L.A. For that reason he didn't really take a huge interest in dating.

Then he met Taylor.

Nash actually first met her right after he moved to L.A. He had been hanging out in the main house where the secret club was located. He was in the house's music studio, messing around with the producer Legacy. Dominic "Legacy" Thomas was part of the rap duo New Boyz, which put out a couple of successful studio albums.

Dom makes these really amazing beats.

Also hanging out in the studio, listening and watching Dom produce, was Taylor Giavasis, Stas's longtime friend.

It's funny that was Taylor's first image of me: making music. I made people laugh, but I'd never

TAYLOR HITCHIN' A RIDE

made music before. I'm never going to put music out
as an artist, but it's part of my general philosophy
of learning every part of my craft and creating my
own opportunities. So, you won't hear my tracks
on top 40 but I'm going to put sound out, make
noise. If I make any music, it'll be to create a
score for movies or scenes.

In that moment, at the big house in the Hollywood Hills right after Nash's arrival in California, music producing was a totally new thing for him. He was just dipping his toes into recording and mixing music tracks. And Taylor was in the room the entire time as he was just learning and exploring. There's some meaning in the fact that her first impression of Nash was while he was trying something new.

It took a year, though, after that afternoon before Taylor and Nash first talked. Stas, who introduced Nash to pretty much everything and everyone in L.A., including Taylor, hung out with her all the time. She, Stas, and Jordyn Woods were tight with one another and together all the time. Jordyn, who was also part of Kylie Jenner's crew, is a plus-size model who stands up for "loving yourself and loving your body," which is something Taylor is all about.

Taylor's body positivity was one of the first things Nash learned about her, because he was familiar with the Instagram account she'd started called the Naked Diaries, which highlights real photos of real people's bodies. It all started with Taylor photographing a friend of hers to make her feel good about her body. The result was that her friend *did* wind up feeling better about herself. That motivated Taylor to do the same for women—and men—of all shapes, sizes, colors.

As her Instagram page quickly grew in popularity, she crystallized her goal for it, which was to embrace "imperfection" in this age of mass proliferation of retouched images. That means, instead of hiding cellulite, extra hair, acne, scars, or rolls, highlighting them. "Real beauty is what makes you unique," she told *People.* "It's curves, stretch marks, moles, laugh lines, skinny and thick legs. I want to depict the beauty of uniqueness, and hopefully teach people they should celebrate what they think their flaws are."

She'll reach out to people wherever she's traveling. She'll meet up with people who have negative self-image issues and talk to them about their entire history. She's teaching people to learn that their imperfections are what make them perfect.

Never was her message more important than in the social media age, when the pressure to live up to a very specific image is immense. Taylor wanted people to worry less about getting "likes" and learning to like themselves—saggy boobs, body hair, and all. It was all about loving yourself, and for that, she gets a lot of love in return, to the tune of 565,000 followers and counting.

Nash stumbled on to Taylor's Instagram page, and was really into the whole thing.

Dang, that's some deep stuff, I thought as I looked at all the beautiful pictures she'd posted.

Although people were exposed, literally, she portrayed them as confident and elegant. Many of the images were accompanied by long, thoughtful captions about each unique story.

So one of the very first things Nash learned about Taylor was something you don't see very often—if at all. She'd started her own movement, and he thought that was really cool. More than cool, it was attractive.

Eventually, Stas and Jordyn introduced Nash to Taylor properly, which meant if he bumped into her at someone's house or at an event, he could say "Hey."

Whenever I saw her, she just kind of had her own vibe, and I was very much digging it. Her almond-shaped black eyes were really fierce and seemed to dare me to get to know her.

They ended up talking a bunch. That's how it started. It was really as simple as "What do you think about this?" or "I'd like to hear more about that." They talked for hours and hours and hours about everything from animal rights and social media to the best places to go dancing, all this different stuff.

It's a cliché to say, but we clicked instantly. If she hadn't come into my life when she did, it could have been very scary. We're dysfunctional when we're not together.

Their relationship started organically. They didn't go out of their way to do anything. Instead they just kind of came together more and more. In the back of her head, she wanted to see him more; in the back of his head, he wanted to see her more.

Inspiring me, she shined a new light on a bunch of stuff and taught me a lot. Taylor definitely fit with everything that I liked and loved. When you like someone and they like you, it's natural that you'll start to spend more time together, which is what we did. We were hanging out more and more with every day that passed. But nothing else about my life was normal, so I doubted Taylor could be normal, either.

The whole time they were getting to know each other, Nash was having so many doubts.

I hope she doesn't kill me.

I hope she's not crazy.

I hope I don't regret this.

It wasn't like there were red flags. It was just the opposite. Nash felt completely safe and calm with her. It was *too* perfect. That's what got him nervous. It was too perfect with Taylor to be real.

Nash's mistrust had nothing to do with Taylor and everything to do with him. He was almost paranoid. Everywhere he went in public, people were pointing their cameras at him. Since moving to L.A., he couldn't go shopping, to the grocery store, anywhere in public without it turning into a photo shoot, and he wasn't always ready for a photo shoot! He hardly went out in public. If he did go anywhere, it was to the beach—alone. Sometimes he hung out at one of his close friends' houses, but other than that, he wouldn't leave the house. He barely went anywhere.

That was the backdrop for Taylor entering Nash's life. The idea of letting someone in definitely took some getting used to. He had met so many phonies since coming to California, how could he tell if anyone was trustworthy? Well, he did his best to figure out if Taylor was.

I decided to study her, like a lab specimen. I pushed her buttons to figure out how she was wired and who she actually is down deep, past her descriptions

*of herself or everyday conversations. You can always
be told something, but until you go out and seek
the information yourself, you'll never really know. So
I did my own investigation. What I discovered was
that I wasn't only attracted to her, she could also
keep me interested. She had things to teach me about
myself, the world, and life.*

Taylor also passed the most important test of all—approval from Nash's mom.

*My mom fell in love with Taylor, which sealed the
deal for me.*

If she could go back home to North Carolina with him, and have his family not only genuinely like but also love her, well, then, it was all good.

*My mom can read people better than anyone else I
know. I trust her judgment above all else.*

There wasn't a moment in time that Nash could point to as the start of their relationship. It happened gradually. After a few years of real loneliness, he was ready for companionship. He didn't have his mom out in L.A. or any feeling of security.

I missed the intelligence and wisdom of women.

Despite the fact that he was so happy and contented to find Taylor, one of the things that Nash stayed away from was promoting the relationship. They never made it a superpublic thing. It's not as if they hid it. They just didn't advertise it.

Smooth, easy, and not over-the-top, it was a real relationship. And the most perfect thing I could ask for.

That is what Nash wanted, to have someone in his life in such a natural way, although he didn't know it before it happened. But it was never about the label—having a girlfriend or being someone's boyfriend.

WITH TAYLOR IN WEST VIRGINIA IN DECEMBER 2018

Taylor and Nash were just trying to live their lives. And that's it. But a year after being together, Nash finally posted something about them being a couple. This wasn't really news since there had already been plenty of coverage and rumors floating around on the internet. The paparazzi took pictures of them that seemed to confirm their relationship status. Everyone (who cared about this kind of thing) already knew they were dating, so at a certain point it began to feel to Nash as if he *were* hiding something by not admitting to it. And Nash didn't want to hide anything. He was proud of his girlfriend and what they had, so he went to Instagram to express it as best he could.

I've always been told Love isn't something you find— Love is something that finds you & I can definitely say that is the case. This is my best friend. We've been together for over a year now. She's one of the most amazing people I've ever met.

He went on to describe his emotional trajectory.

Eventually I was able to clear my mind & spend some time with this girl & I'm so thankful I did. As we started hanging out we developed more & more of a trust for each other, one that continues to change my life for the better. As I begin to describe her (& our relationship) all words seem to lose meaning & don't really do any justice.

MULTITASKING

No matter how hard I try to put together a sequence of words/feelings nothing will be able explain my love for this girl. Taylor—Thank you for being you. You've changed my life in SO many ways & I'm so blessed to have you. You've opened up a new world for me, whether it be the new perspectives I can now see from or the new feelings/ emotions I get every day when I'm with you. You continue to make me the best person I can be just by being yourself. Whether we're flying overseas or sitting on the couch you never fail to make me the happiest person I've ever been. Everything about you is such an inspiration—From your free spirit & your beautiful soul to the words that come out of your mouth you've always been a gift to the world. Thank you for selflessly spreading your divine energy & messages. You are changing this world one person at a time & I'm so thankful I'm one of those people, love you.

Undoubtedly, my favorite thing about my relationship with Taylor is that we learn things from each other all the time. Equally motivated about what we want to do and who we want to be, we support each other in our individual paths.

Part of the reason Nash and Taylor decided to live together after he left the Valley was that each of them had a notebook full of goals, dreams, and ideas that they wanted to do for the next year. Comparing notes, they both felt there was no one else with whom either of them could achieve those dreams. And they definitely wouldn't do them alone. So they took a yearlong lease on a house on the beach and moved in together.

We moved away from everyone to a one bedroom, one bathroom on top of a canyon in Malibu. We didn't have a car, and Uber wouldn't even come out there! It was a good hour and a half from Hollywood. It was almost like a retreat. Other than the commute, we were living our best life.

Taylor was Nash's first real, actual relationship. Before her, he didn't know what a relationship was. Not really. He paid attention to his stepdad and mom, and knew they had a special connection. But it wasn't until he felt that connection with another human being himself that he really understood. Love is the most powerful thing on the planet. Through Taylor, he was able to take the first step to really growing up.

MOVING DAY

When I'm with Taylor, my life is better. I laugh more, smile more, learn more. I get all this cool stuff. I fell in love with her, and I still fall in love with her. Every day there's a new reason why I like her this much more. She's taught me patience, what matters and what doesn't. We grow as a pair.

NASH'S

PLACES TRAVELED

U.S.A.!!! lol 😄 Hawaii, N.Y., L.A., Miami, etc. etc. 🇺🇸

Canada 🇨🇦

Mexico 🇲🇽

Belize 🇧🇿

Peru 🇵🇪

Argentina 🇦🇷

Brazil 🇧🇷

Chile 🇨🇱

Jamaica 🇯🇲

South Africa 🇿🇦

French Polynesia 🇵🇫

Iceland 🇮🇸

United Kingdom 🇬🇧

United Arab Emirates 🇦🇪

Czech Republic 🇨🇿

Georgia 🇬🇪

France 🇫🇷

Portugal 🇵🇹

Swaziland 🇸🇿

Puerto Rico 🇵🇷

Italy 🇮🇹

Indonesia 🇮🇩

Australia 🇦🇺

CHAPTER 11

Nash learned exponentially more in the past several years since he left home than he did for the first sixteen years of his life. It's been crazy what he was able to see and do in terms of real-life experiences—and not just in love and social media but also in business and building his brand.

Part of his huge learning curve when he first arrived in L.A. came from taking meetings with some of the biggest companies *ever*. Nash was invited into massive corporations to help inform them about *his* space and how they could grow in it. In board-rooms filled with guys in suits, CEOs and geniuses of traditional media and advertising asked Nash—a sixteen-year-old kid in a T-shirt, jeans, and baseball cap—for insight. It was strange. He knew what he did, and knew it well. But he wasn't necessarily sure how he played a role in selling stuff for big businesses that have whole departments for just that very thing.

I definitely didn't want to be part of any mass marketing campaign for something people didn't need or want. What I noticed as both a consumer and content creator was that whenever companies wanted to send out a message about their stuff, it wasn't intimate. No matter how "cool" or informal they tried to make them, their ads always felt like just that: commercials. An email shoved in your face over and over is just as bad as "Call 1-800-blah, blah, blah. Right now!!!" or "Side effects may include . . ."

Many brands struggle with how to connect to an audience, and it's not necessarily because their product is bad, or wrong, or anything. (Of course, there are certain products and companies that are bad, and because of the internet and more access to information, people are more aware of their bad practices, whether it be polluting or animal cruelty.) But the way many established companies are trying to reach customers, particularly young ones, is just flat-out wrong.

Kids these days aren't stupid. They laugh at commercials just like Nash does. He finds them hilarious—in a pathetic ShamWow kind of way. The things that they try to sell on TV are all in a particular arena. Cars, cable companies, insurance, pills. Okay, maybe they can persuade some older people in thirty seconds to switch to Geico or pop some Viagra. But with kids? No way.

We think those ads are ridiculous and good for making funny GIFs. That's not how you get us interested in what you're selling, and that's not how I want to be promoting anything at all.

Nash received a lot of offers to promote products but was very selective with the ones he accepted. Whether it was a carrier brand for phones, bottled water, or an awards show, he wanted to endorse stuff that was innovative, unique, and cool.

At least to me, because that's the only person I can really claim to speak for.

That's the core of his marketing philosophy: he is not going to put anything out there that he wouldn't use, eat, watch, or wear himself. The relationship with the people who watch his stuff is so authentic, because there's nothing that's too personal for him to put on social media. What makes him feel good about what he does, and what he knows his followers appreciate too, is that it's all 100 percent real. Emotions, thoughts, everything.

Even if I change how I think or feel later, everything is true in the moment.

Because Nash's followers belong to a very different culture than the one that tunes into network TV, they have to be accessed in a different way. You can't do what so many brands want to do, which is say "This is a script for our campaign. Let's send it to all these influencers and have them post it." That's the worst thing you can do. When people see the same posts on more than one site, they know instantly it's fake.

Other social media influencers get called out for putting up posts for teeth whiteners, diet teas, wrinkle filler, and any other ubiquitous, bogus product. Nash has never done that, and never will.

I have too much respect for my followers.

Every influencer is different. It's just like personalities—no two are exactly alike.

I still struggle with being an influencer; I'm not better or smarter than anyone.

Nash's page will never be the same as someone else's, because it's his. What makes the internet so unique is that to be a part of it, you have to dive into it and spend some time there. No one, other than the influencer who has the audience and the audience that appreciates the influencer, knows the hows and whys of accessing their collective space. That's why if Nash is going to promote a product, it has to be in his voice and in his way.

One example of this was the promotion Nash did with M&M's. In 2015, the candy company Mars decided to bring back Crispy M&M's, which had been discontinued ten years earlier. Fans had organized an online campaign with petitions and tweets to bring them back. So the company reached out to Nash to see if they could do a deal.

Nash was interested in working with M&M's, because he actually ate them.

This was before I went vegan. Pretzel M&M's are fire; peanut M&M's are fire.

This could be a good fit, but only if the company agreed to a few things.

"If you want me to access my audience, I can't just flash some stupid ad in front of them that says, 'Here! Eat these!'" Nash said. "No. If we really want conversion, then it needs to be a campaign. Maybe we can brainstorm. I've got some cool ideas of how we can partner."

They were into it, and as a gesture of goodwill sent what might as well have been a lifetime supply of Crispy M&M's to his house in L.A. Crispy M&M's were indeed fire!

After talking it out, Mars and Nash agreed on a plan—which entailed him flying out to New York for a couple of days to do a press tour on a lot of the major media outlets, like *Good Morning America* and *Today*. That was nice, but most important, he was getting his fan base together in New York.

Nash had done meet-ups in New York before, including full-on festivals, gatherings in Central Park, and one at Citi Field, where more than twenty thousand people showed up to this Queens stadium, which is home to the Mets, to meet him.

I just have a very cool audience that is always on the go in New York. These kids will drop everything to come to the airport as soon as I land, the morning station I'm at, or wherever. They say New

*Yorkers have an attitude but I've never received
anything other than warm hugs and lots of love
in the Big Apple. Because of that, New York is a
place I've gone back to many times over the years,
and where, just like in Toronto, L.A., and Chicago,
I've grown my engaged and awesome audience into a
family. It's really cool.*

While Nash was in New York for Crispy M&M's, Mars gave him a giant truck that was only a little smaller than a semi. On its side was an enormous image of him holding some M&M's with the line "Nash Has Crispy."

*It was sick. So I'm riding around New York in
this monster vehicle, just tossing Crispy M&M's to
everybody like Willy Wonka on wheels.*

They were en route to a meet-up they had announced, which was free. No one had to do anything but show up. Although it was a school day, six thousand people came to the pier where it was held for a huge meet and greet, where everyone got pictures, Crispy M&M's, T-shirts, and other swag. There was music going on, and it felt just like a real outdoor party.

M&M's went out of its way to give that to his fans—and not only was it amazing for his followers, it was also amazing for Mars. To this day, Nash's fans still love M&M's and still post pictures from that day of them wearing a T-shirt they got at the event. That's on top of all the footage and photos he took and posted, and that were reposted. If he had two million followers on Snapchat, it was easy to imagine at least 100,000 of them taking a screenshot of a picture he took with M&M's from that day. That meant, instantly, 100,000 people now had a picture of Nash with M&M's on their iCloud and every single one of their devices. That's a lot of product placement for M&M's.

As brands learn more and more about how to engage and use social media, they are getting more specific in their negotiations. There are ways that haven't even been thought out on how to market in social media, and people are still learning it. But no matter how you push the message out, for any promotion to work it always has to align with the true interests of the influencer and engage his or her audience in an authentic way.

Nash has learned so much about marketing since starting his career. No matter what it is—from M&M's to movies—he can take any brand or product and envision the best way to market it. He's seen so many brands and had so many people contact him to discuss this campaign or that promotion. But everything he does must fit with what he believes in and what his brand stands for.

Everything I say has to be 100 percent authentic.

That doesn't just include products he lends his name or audience to, but also ones he invests in. Investing is something Nash is kind of new to, but he hopes to do more with business ventures he believes in, such as those creating clean energy. He wants to invest in solar and wind power and make his dollars count toward making clean water accessible all over the world and ending world hunger.

These are goals that I believe are achievable in this lifetime.

Nash has worked on a bunch of apps. A lot of his deals have been with apps and social networks, testing out which ones will work and trying to figure out the future of social media. It's fascinating to be able to learn about and try out these new technologies firsthand. It's like doing a real-life experiment. Nash even made his own app, and got 200,000 people on there in a couple of days!

He also made a game called Cash Dash, which got a million downloads in a day. The platformer-styled game featured Cameron Dallas; Carter Reynolds, who's also from North Carolina; Nash's brother Hayes, who has followed in his footsteps and by the age of thirteen already had 3 million followers on Vine, more than 2.6 million on Instagram, and over 1.5 million on Twitter; and, of course, Nash. Players could choose any one of the social media stars to beat each of the game's seventy levels in three minutes or less to win badges and shoot to the top of the global leaderboard. The pretty classic app—where you have to kill the bad guys (like mummies) by shooting them or jumping on them—went to number one on the App Store.

The idea was that those at the top of the leaderboard had the best shot at being followed by Cam, Nash, or the rest of the guys. But they also communicated with everyone who signed up for the game, by sending fan mail and merch letters. That was a true interaction with their fans. That's how it works. It's a give-and-take relationship. Everyone is growing with one another. There's a real purpose and point to this.

It's not just about me throwing some crap onto my social media. We're actually creating a journey that we go on together.

It's the same spirit of collaboration that drove Nash early on to create a collab page for the original MagCon crew. You never know what can happen when you're willing to work with others. If you had told him that he could direct a music video, Nash would have laughed. But a year after moving to L.A., that's exactly what he did. And again, the opportunity to do the video came about from another connection through his dad. This time it was the remarkable Georgian artist, Bera.

Bera Ivanishvili is as cool as his one-of-a-kind look. An albino, his platinum white hair and skin stands in contrast to his tough style. So does the fact that although he's known for his rap and club music, he's actually a classically trained musician with perfect pitch. Born in Paris (although his roots are in the Republic of Georgia), he started violin at five years old and piano two years later. By sixteen, he launched his own record label, Georgian Dream, and was putting out albums with the same producers who worked with Lady Gaga and Michael Jackson.

Nash heard of Bera before they met in person, not only because he was out in L.A. recording music, but because he had

PARIS FASHION WEEK WITH BERA AND FRENCH
MODEL BAPTISTE GIABICONI

also hosted a 2014 VMA pre-party with Kendall and Kylie Jenner and a bunch of other folks. Still, Nash wasn't sure what he was going to get when he met this guy. A rich party boy? A wannabe gangsta rapper?

I had made it a practice to avoid drama and was wary of unknown entities like Bera.

As soon as they met and started talking, though, Nash was bowled over by Bera and his story. His father, Bidzina Ivanishvili, had been prime minister of Georgia. Bera had put his own life in jeopardy by performing at important political rallies during the 2012 election in order to get young Georgians to come out and vote.

So much stuff went off in my head from a creator perspective that I said to myself, "Damn! I need to tell this guy's story."

Despite their very different life stories, Bera and Nash had a lot in common. They shared a similar point of view on work. Just as Nash is involved in every aspect of what he does, from writing and production to editing and promotion, Bera knows how to do everything from recording and mastering to marketing. "You have to be on top of everything in today's music industry climate," said Bera, whose music is influenced by everyone from jazz greats to Notorious B.I.G. and Lionel Richie. Nash loved the eclectic nature of Bera's passions. But even more than Bera's diverse musical interests, Nash appreciated and related to his attitude toward fame. Bera is ambitious, but his heart is in the right place. As Bera says on his website, "When someone thinks about me or my music, I want them to smile. I don't need to be a superstar. I don't want to be that untouchable guy. I want to be like you, and I want you to feel my music and enjoy it with me. I just want to share my feelings."

Nash wanted to tell Bera's story. However, he was shocked when Bera asked him to direct a music video for him. The song, "I Look Good on You," is a fun, feel-good dance tune that came to Bera quickly while jamming with his crew. Nash wanted the video, shot entirely in black and white, to reflect that vibe. He recruited his own crew, his bro Hayes, Jack & Jack, Sammy, the musician and *X Factor* USA runner up Wesley Stromberg, and Vine star Jake Foushee, who all pretended to play instruments. They brought a lot of energy and the party vibe he wanted to capture.

"It was a great experience, because first of all, I think it was a learning process for both of us," Bera has said about his collaboration with Nash. "He introduced me to the social media world and taught me things that I didn't know, and I think I introduced him to the music world."

This great new friendship and making a music video were just two of the many things Nash never dreamed would be part of his career. Another one was fashion.

His foray into the industry began with Paris Fashion Week in the fall of 2015. Designers hit Nash up for a deal, and he traveled to France for his first-ever fashion week, which Bera was also attending. During that trip, Nash had the great honor of attending Vivienne Westwood's show. If you don't know this seminal British designer, you should. The Queen of Punk began designing clothes in the 1970s when she opened her shop first called Let It Rock, and then later, Sex. There, Westwood, who dressed the Sex Pistols, practically created the classic punk look, which included spiked dog collar chokers, safety pins, plaid, leather, and spiky hair.

Known for pushing boundaries (in 2003, she sent men down the runway of one of her shows wearing fake breasts), Westwood is just as radical now as she was when she started out. She's one of Nash's favorite designers, ever. He was totally psyched to see her show—and even more psyched when he was invited backstage afterward to talk to the legend face-to-face. Before they were introduced, her manager briefed him on the subjects that interested her, such as climate change and geopolitics.

"Oh, really?" Nash said. "That's what I'm interested in, too."

The young social media star and veteran designer wound up talking backstage for about an hour, until it was really time to leave.

We talked about climate change!

As if spending all that time with Nash right after something as important as showing her fashion collection weren't enough, Westwood also sent him a pair of boots she made!

Paris represented Nash dipping his toe into fashion, which was a really important moment. During that trip, he made some amazing connections with designers, stylists, fabric makers—all kinds of really creative people. That was crucial because, as with entertainment, connections and relationships are everything in fashion. Relationships are how that whole thing works.

One of his first forays into this world was signing with one of the biggest modeling agencies in the world, with offices in London, New York, Paris, Milan, Los Angeles, and Miami. In addition to models, they also represent a lot of general talent with fashion clout. Nash signed with the agency almost as soon as he got home, because they were eager to promote him in the industry and book him at more fashion weeks, both in Europe and New York—and not just walking in shows. Nash did a deal at New York Fashion Week for Tommy Hilfiger, pegged to the return of Tommy jeans. Nash was hired to wear his clothes to the fashion show, where he sat in the front row and then posted about it afterward.

Nash was one of the few among his social media crew who was really into fashion.

I love the environment of the runway. Everything from the venue, set design, lighting, the music, to the way you enter, who you are sitting beside. It's pure adrenaline when the music starts pumping and you take to the runway. Even just watching a show, seeing someone's vision—and the work of a lot of craftspeople—come to life is a special thing. The best shows curate every little detail of the entire show exactly how they want, making it more of an experience than a show.

Eventually, if Nash can put together the right message with the right production, he hopes to create his own clothing line. One of his inspirations is Ugo Mozie—who is already a huge name in fashion at twenty-five years old. Ugo moved to New York City from Texas when he was seventeen, and just two years later, he debuted his own fashion line, Aston Mozie. In addition to his design skills, Ugo's a stylist who has worked with such stars as Chris Brown, Beyoncé, and Kelly Rowland. From movies to magazines, Ugo's reach is felt. It's no wonder that Vivienne Westwood hired Ugo to work in PR for her company.

Ugo made me a custom hat, a beautiful Carolina blue with a nice brim.

Nash loves clothes that are both daring and put-together—and which are ultimately very personal. Fashion week has every kind of crazy combination, from someone in snowboard boots, shorts, and a fancy blouse to a guy in a three-piece suit and bowler hat. No matter whether it's a sweatshirt or neon stilettos, these people are practiced in the art of communicating something about themselves through their clothes. It doesn't matter if they are completely breaking the "rules." If they are living their expression, they look amazing.

But what about Nash's style? When he first started to blow up, Nash pretty much had the same clothes as every other fourteen-year-old kid in America. When he went to a meet and greet, he'd wear an Obey or Zumiez T-shirt or something from Tillys. Normal stuff that everybody has, except when he wore it, pictures of him in that shirt were plastered all over the internet. So when he saw pictures online of someone else in the same shirt, it was embarrassing. At least to him.

Damn, I'm boring, I thought. I suck.

Nash's style was yet another thing he had to figure out after his life changed overnight. He went from wearing bow ties and collared shirts—aka dressing like a lacrosse-playing private school kid—to being able to dress however he wanted. Without rules and guidelines, he no longer had to wear bow ties on game days. Although he had the freedom to wear whatever he wanted, he still wasn't able to afford the clothes that he wanted to wear. Instead, Nash wore whatever he could get his hands on—in other words, the same shirts as every other kid in every other mall in America.

Nash was met with backlash for his choice of T-shirts or hairstyle. "Why is Nash Grier trying to be Harry Styles?" people asked when he grew his hair long. He wasn't trying to be anyone else. Like everyone else, Nash was just getting up and getting dressed every morning (and not cutting his hair). But he no longer had the luxury of *not* thinking about his look.

Whenever Nash went outside, there were a bunch of cameras on him. He had to wear something that was forty years old so nobody else would be seen in it, too.

> I like stuff that's vintage. If there's a history to the piece or material it's just cooler. Honestly. There are more colors in it. It's more random. Older stuff is more daring. The rules are kind of lost with clothing as it gets older and older.

Nash started to shop at thrift stores, Goodwill, and American Vintage. Wherever there was old stuff, like a one-of-a-kind flannel jacket or a bowling shirt.

> I don't care if it belonged to someone three years ago, just as long as no one has it right now. I would do anything to not be compared to someone else, or look like someone else. I'd rather be naked than wear the same clothes as someone else. I've had school unis before, not doing that again.

Buying old clothes was a quick-fix solution. What really bothered Nash, however, ran a lot deeper. It upset him how many small stereotypes are employed, and make an impact, because people don't think of them as stereotypes. In this way, fashion is a metaphor for a lot in life. For example, Nash doesn't really get why there is a division between guys' clothing and girls' clothing.

That really tripped me up when I started going to fashion shows. How can you even say that this is meant for guys, and this is meant for girls? I get the underwear, I guess. But forget the underwear piece for a sec. How can you say this is a guy's shirt, or this is a girl's shirt? Or this is a men's hoodie, or a women's? That whole thing was a head-scratcher to me. Experimentation in dressing isn't new by any means, yet nearly every collection and even the fashion week seasons are divided into men's and women's. I suppose that's just a money thing—in that case, though, start a unisexual fashion week and promote that as well. There's too many people and too much creativity for everybody to be looking the same.

Nash believes a man should be able to wear a dress if he wants to—as a shirt or as a . . . dress! He could even wear heels if that feels right. A young woman should be able to wear a dope sweat suit to her prom. Clothes should just be clothes, without any issues of sexuality or sexual identity getting in the way of expression.

People need to accept who they are and not hide under clothes. Most outfits are just uniforms, whether it's Ugg boots or the kind of frat-boy clothing Nash used to wear. It stems from this external voice saying "You need to fit in." There's way too much of that.

We need to lose this notion of what is socially correct in terms of dressing and stop safely segregating ourselves into stereotypes.

If there weren't these guidelines, we would all look very different from how we do now. In Nash's vision for the future, which is very much his own and not necessarily popular, we would all be expressing ourselves in our own way.

All these crazy thoughts about clothes, personal expression, and his own future started in Paris. There he hung out with Bera, who has a lot of connections in the fashion industry. By making a few well-placed calls, Bera got Nash into five or six more shows. It was while they were at one of these shows, Maison Margiela, that Bera turned to Nash and said, "Hey, after fashion week, why don't you come with me to Georgia?"

So far, Bera hadn't steered him wrong, so Nash answered, "Sure. Why not?"

CHAPTER 12

The trip to Georgia with Bera was yet another course in the education of Nash Grier.

I don't even know where to begin.

Georgia, situated in between Russia, Turkey, and Armenia, is a small country with a population of less than five million people. Touching the Black Sea, it is a dividing line between Asia and Europe and is considered by some the motherland of Europe. The people are extremely proud, and the land is extremely beautiful. The rugged peaks of the Caucasus Mountains and the coastal towns have always attracted visitors from the earliest times—including the thirteenth-century explorer Marco Polo.

Georgia fell under Soviet rule in the twentieth century, but after the Soviet Union broke up in the '90s, the country went through a period of great turmoil. That's where Bera's family enters the story. The life of Bera's dad, Bidzina, could be a whole movie in itself. He is Georgia's richest man, with an estimated worth of $6.4 billion.

Although he is something like the 153rd-richest person on the planet, Bidzina started out life extremely poor. The youngest of five kids, he was born in the rural Georgia village of Chorvila, where he had to literally walk through frozen fields to school in hand-me-down boots with no socks. Still, he graduated from high school in the top of his class and went on to get a Ph.D. in economics in Moscow, where he ultimately made his fortune. He ran his first importing business from a three-room apartment, and made enough money to start a bank that he opened in a corner of a kindergarten!

Although Bidzina made it big in Russia, he decided to return to his home country, where he lives in a crazy $40-million complex that took more than a decade to build. Made out of glass and steel and known as the "James Bond house," there is a helipad on the roof, a man-made waterfall, and a giant rotating steel ball inside a glass tower that contains a private café suspended above a swimming pool. As if that isn't enough, it also contains one of the most valuable art collections in the world, including a Picasso he bought in 2006 for almost $100 million.

I realize that makes him sound like some Bond villain. In reality, Bidzina is a superhumble guy. And I don't mean like look-how-humble-I-am fake humble.

He is truly a to-himself kind of guy who never gives interviews. (In fact, there are only a few photos of him out there on the internet; that's how private he is.) The only way he originally made his presence known in Georgia is through the many public projects he funded, such as a seaside amusement park, a ski resort, national parks, and medical clinics.

That is, until he entered the political sphere. Bidzina wound up using his massive wealth to create a new political party, Georgian Dream, whose mission was to overthrow the ruling party in parliamentary elections. But it wasn't just his millions that got him elected prime minister of Georgia in 2012, in a huge upset victory. Part of it had to do with videos he released that exposed abuse of prison inmates. Ultimately, voters were moved by his honesty.

Bera was by his dad's side the whole way. He released a song called "Georgian Dream" to support his father's campaign, which he performed, despite threats to him, at election rallies.

Everything Nash learned, saw, tasted, drank, danced, and experienced on his trip in Georgia was eye-opening. He went to places built at the time that Jesus walked the earth. He learned that the country has its own ancient alphabet. Nash was lucky to have a tour guide as integral to the history of the land as Bera, who remains his great friend to this day.

I told him I will return to Georgia one day, because I want to direct something on his life. Whether it's a feature-length narrative movie or a documentary, what his family has done and what he continues to do has to be told.

I know most people don't have access to folks like Bera when they go abroad, but that doesn't matter. I definitely feel like every person who lives in the United States has to get out of the country and see places far beyond their comfort zone. The more you travel the more you realize it's all home.

Experiencing new places, personally seeing how different nature, architecture, and human beings are across this earth, is one of the best things you can do for yourself. Nash loves to travel whenever he can. Events, meet and greets, hosting award shows, fashion shows, festivals, whatever the excuse, he jumps at the opportunity. On top of that, he sets up his own adventures or trips, based off his interests, like snowboarding in Breckenridge and Keystone, Colorado, or surfing in Hawaii.

One of the crucial elements for him when he travels is *not* to be a tourist. Anywhere you go, there's going to be the tourism side of it, and then there's going to be the authentic culture. Unfortunately, more often than not those two sides are in opposition. Classic tourism can feed into systems of greed that exploit the land and people in order to make money.

Plus, you don't get on a plane so that you can listen to some guy shouting from a bus and then buy some crap you don't need from a trinket shop.

The only way to travel is to meet and hang out with the locals. That's why if Nash is traveling someplace—like Hawaii—he tries to plan a meet-up there, too. It's an opportunity to establish a fan base in new places, but it also gives him the fuel for everything that he posts and does while there. Having fun, meeting people, and making content is the essence of what Nash does. Doing it in faraway places is just the icing on the cake.

For example, Nash did a free meet-up in Georgia during the two weeks he spent there with Bera. They booked a movie theater with a 3,500-person capacity and announced the event two days in advance: "Hey, come meet us. We're going to be onstage performing." Nash had already directed the video for "I Look Good on You," so he and Bera performed the hit song together to a packed house. The audience went absolutely crazy.

The people Nash met didn't speak English all that well, and his Georgian was practically nonexistent. Still, they were able to have a real exchange, as Nash indulged himself in Georgian culture. The more he learned about the natives of this land, the more excited he felt about the place.

> I wanted to meet more and more people. It became a passion to meet and talk to them, not only to learn about the cool places to hang out but also to hear their reactions and feel their emotions.

Each one of the trips Nash has taken has had such a huge impact on him. By showing him a completely new way of life, travel has helped to create who he is as a person. It could be a trip for weeks or just a couple of days, but as long as he gets the vibe of what it's like to live in the place—from the food to the clothing and the music—then Nash is changed by the new perspective.

In Hawaii, Nash learned how proud locals are of their land and the reverence they show in the way they treat it. This is in contrast to outsiders who just want to industrialize and destroy the natural beauty of that amazing place. Despite the history of the white man—who basically took over what had been an independent kingdom, brought new diseases, and eventually forced statehood on it—Nash was treated graciously when he visited. They put leis and beads all over him and served him all these amazing Hawaiian foods and fruits. As if that weren't enough, the people he met on this trip vowed, "We're going to take you to all the cool spots." And they did. But more important, they shared with him their painful history of corporations monetizing places like Honolulu and industrializing natural, sacred habitats.

Before Nash arrived, he already had fans to guide him in Hawaii. But anyone can learn a lot just by talking and listening to the people who actually live in the place they're visiting. If you're shy, you don't even need to talk to people—just look around and observe.

When I went to France, I was struck by how they didn't knock buildings down once they get old. In the United States, if a building is more than fifty years old, we feel the need to destroy it and make a new one. In France, though, they like to preserve their architecture. Walking down the street, I marveled at the beauty all around me. Every single

SELFIE WITH FANS IN THE AIRPORT AFTER
TOUCHING DOWN IN MILAN IN 2018

apartment building, bridge, and storefront was unique
in its layers of history.

Anytime Nash is traveling for an event or pleasure, he loves
bringing his camera and documenting the journey. Sometimes
he'll see an image and think, *Oh, yes! That's the perfect moment to
tell the whole story of the trip.* Even if he doesn't post it, he loves
having the visual to jog the entire memory of the experience. So
the camera becomes another way for him to engage with a place.
But certain times when he's traveling, he puts down all his electronic devices so that he can have a pure experience.

When Nash went to Joshua Tree National Park for a three-
day cleanse of the soul, that's exactly what he did. Every place he's

traveled to is unique, and Joshua Tree's stark desert terrain, less than three hours from L.A., was no exception. With no cell service, no electricity or running water, Nash and a group of like-minded people spent their time hiking, writing, looking at the stars, and reflecting. They stood on top of plateaus, looking as far as the eye could see. And within that distance, there was not a single human or sign of civilization, not a pipeline or plastic bag. Nothing but beautiful, untouched land, and really, really, really hot sun.

We were in the middle between earth and sky.

Nash brought his camera, with which he filmed a video, but just his camera. For that entire trip, and the four days leading up to it, he put his phone down. That was not just a hiatus to posting; that was him not communicating with anyone; that was him exiling himself electronically.

Even as an influencer, I've put my phone down for weeks at a time. I don't do it often, but if I really want to get something done, have some quality creative time, I'll do it. Plus, being unreachable by dropping off the map for a period feels good.

There's a quality of life that's different when you're not on electronics. Experiencing the world though a screen versus without one is obviously radically different. The screen represents an intermediary layer. As interactive as a lot of our devices may seem, on a certain level they're the opposite. Life outside of the virtual world, the screen, a movie, TV—it's not predetermined. That's the biggest factor.

Everything in real life happens in real time. You stand here. The other person walks over there. You break the rules. Someone else doesn't break the rules. Body language, spoken language. Action, reaction. That's life: it happens.

Meanwhile, everything that's going on the internet is pretty much predetermined before it goes up. You decide what words to use and what picture to put up—even what name to use. You decide the story, the image, the content. It doesn't always play out as you planned or hoped—sometimes there is a backlash or something goes viral, neither of which you might have expected. Still, you have time to craft your response.

The internet is whatever you want it to be. You can be whatever you want. Nash could hide behind any account he wanted to. He could take on any identity. There might not even be a Nash Grier, for all people know.

Don't worry, there is.

The flip side of this level of contrivance is that the internet can also become whatever you don't want it to be. There's also the whole negative side of online content.

Nash experiences a lot of new things through screens, but sometimes even he needs a break—especially being in L.A., where real life itself can sometimes feel like a screen. There are a lot of places in California that are really good for that—like Joshua Tree, Big Sur, or Sequoia National Park. Those are some of the spots he escapes to whenever he's overwhelmed and needs to step back and just detox from tech.

As someone who puts so much of himself online, he likes to have points of time here and there when he's not accessible. It's better than always being on, because Nash never wants to overdo that. At the same time, he can't be off social media too much, because then there goes his activation; there goes all the work he's done nearly every day to keep people coming back to his page. But going dark for a week is not going to drive away his loyal fans.

> Sometimes my stuff gets more activation and higher numbers from <u>not</u> posting as much.

While Nash has devoted himself to making content, he differentiates himself from other social media stars, in that many live their entire lives online. There is nothing they don't post. While Nash is 100 percent open with everyone and everything online, he still has things he does or that occur in his life that he does *not* post. Like everything else in life, it is about finding a balance.

You might think that Nash would experience withdrawal when he goes without his phone, but he doesn't.

> I've seen that with other people. It's like they don't know where to look or what to do with their hands. It's almost as if someone amputated one of their limbs. That's not my experience. When I put down the device, instead of feeling bereft, I go back to a simpler, judgment-free time in my life: childhood.

For many years during his childhood, Nash didn't have electronics. Other than watching a few TV shows here and there that his mom put in front of him (probably so she could have a moment to herself), he never had anything—

which I think is great. It helped me figure out what is fun and how to use my imagination.

The lack of imagination that arises from the reliance on electronics is going to be a problem in the future. It's a tricky issue, because on one level the internet and our amazing connectivity help fuel imagination in the infinite possibilities that are opened up on devices to anyone who wants to make movies, music, art, games, or simply communicate. At the same time, though, it also kind of takes imagination away. Especially for kids.

The phone is the most popular toy around. You can see children on them all the time—in restaurants, public transportation, even playgrounds, asking for games.

That worries me. I can see a generation of kids growing up hunched over their phones. What is the evolution of our posture going to be?

Adults are equally addicted to the internet. If your charger breaks, your life stops until you get a new charger. We should be fine without these things. But we're not; we're all dependent. The web is seductive, because it makes it seem like you have everything at your fingertips. But that's simply not true. There are some things we can only understand by picking our heads up and seeing them for ourselves.

That gets me back to traveling, which is the act of seeing how other people—on the same spinning rock we're all on—live. I've gone to a lot of places, but there are still so many more for me to see. No matter where it is that I go—Africa, Asia, South America—I want to not only gain the unique perspective that belongs to the people who live in those places but also spread the best energy and positivity I possibly can.

CHAPTER 13

As a public person, Nash's actions both online and off affect a lot of people—but probably no one more so than his brother Hayes. When Nash took off and left home at sixteen, armed only with the mind-set that he had the ability to create whatever kind of existence he chose for himself, he definitely changed Hayes's life forever.

Nash had his ups and downs in L.A.—from his early loneliness and partying too much to getting fed up with all the projects that were being put in front of him by others and figuring out what he was truly passionate about—but setting the basic example of stepping out of his comfort zone and trusting himself to build a career was enough to inspire his younger brother to do the same.

Hayes becoming a social media star in his own right is an exact parallel to Nash following in Will's footsteps while playing football. When their dad compared Will and Nash's skill levels, Nash was a better football player than his older brother was at that age. Will is a god in the sport. Nash had a leg up even on his older brother *because* he had Will's example to mimic. In the same way, Hayes easily and naturally developed his own content and persona on social media, from watching Nash struggle to make his videos, go to meet and greets, and manage his posts. Whatever advances Nash made on social media, Hayes escalated them.

The whole time Nash was building his career, Hayes was building his own. Their dad managed Nash for a while, which was another reason it just seemed natural for his little brother to be signed to the team as well. If Chad was making deals for one kid, he might as well do it for two. In this way, Hayes started getting thrown into the mix of events, appearances, and paid posts. He joined the MagCon tour in 2014, which included Matthew Espinosa, Carter Reynolds, Aaron Carpenter, Jack & Jack, Cameron Dallas, and others. When Cam, Carter, and Nash made a deal with Aéropostale to promote the United XXVI Summer Collection, a clothing line they helped design, Hayes was a part of that, too.

Because a lot of Nash's audience would flock to his little brother and join his audience, eventually, Hayes was kind of in the same space as his older brother. Although they continue to have a similar following, Hayes is completely different than Nash.

Like I said earlier, he's a wild man, a Tasmanian devil—with a sensitive side. Hayes is crazy as hell and doesn't see anything other than what's right below his feet. While I think I do a pretty good job of having a vision for the future and reminiscing on the past, Hayes just lives for now. In a way, I'm jealous of him, even though I'm very familiar with the disadvantages to his way of being.

Hayes is all over the place. One month, he will be obsessed with an activity, doing whatever it is every minute of every day, only to drop it for something else the next month. Case in point: motocross. When Hayes decided off-road motorcycle racing was his purpose in this life, he scoured Craigslist for old dirt bikes, which he bought and fixed up himself. He even negotiated two new dirt bikes into one of his tour deals, instead of other forms of payment.

I'm not sure that made the best business sense, but when Hayes gets on something, there is no getting him off it.

PLAYING BOX LACROSSE WITH HAYES

So he wound up with six dirt bikes, which he would race all the time. For a while. Then as fast as he falls in love, he falls out of it.

I haven't heard anything about motocross for a while but that's normal. He's still growing and trying to find not only himself and what makes sense as a next step but also what he's passionate about.

That's part of the reason Nash was so impressed with his little brother's run on *Dancing with the Stars*: that was the first time he worked really hard at something and pushed himself past what he thought were his limits.

The *Dancing with the Stars* gig was another example of Hayes following in Nash's footsteps.

Well, in this case, I stepped aside for him.

ABC approached Nash first with an offer to compete in the reality show. Although the network offered Nash more money than he could imagine, it didn't fit with where he wanted to take his career in the moment. Still, the show is so big and can have such an impact, Nash didn't want to throw it away. So he emailed the *Dancing* people back: "What if Hayes did it?"

ABC was into it, but Nash still had to persuade Hayes. At first, he didn't like the idea. At all.

"No. I'm not doing it. No. No!" Hayes said.

Although Hayes can act like a lunatic, he's actually very shy. If you look at any group picture of Hayes from when he was little, like a class or team photo, he's crying, because he doesn't want to be photographed.

There are some really funny pictures of him in full tantrum.

If posing with his second-grade soccer team made Hayes nervous, you can just imagine how joining the cast of *Dancing with the Stars* made him feel. He had never done anything nearly as big as joining the twenty-first season of the hit dance competition show. Not only would he be the youngest contestant the show ever had, but Hayes didn't have the slightest clue how to dance.

Unless you count the white man's overbite at a school dance.

In the end, Nash didn't convince Hayes to dance competitively in front of an audience of millions on national television. Hayes convinced himself. His rationale went something like this: "Free ticket to L.A.? Time out of school? Okay, let's do it."

The next week, I kid you not, Hayes was out in L.A., sleeping on my couch.

To prepare for *Dancing with the Stars*, Hayes had at least ten-hour rehearsals for weeks and weeks. Nash wasn't sure if his baby brother had what it took to stick with it. So much of the power at his fingertips was just given to him, and he hadn't really struggled for much of anything in his life. It wasn't his fault, but he was always either Will or Nash Grier's little brother.

WITH WILL AND
HAYES IN L.A.

THE BROTHERS ATOP
RAVEN'S ROCK, WEST
VIRGINIA

When the competition began, Hayes and his partner, Emma Slater, went in there and killed it. What was so cool about Hayes doing *Dancing with the Stars* was how passionate he got about it. He pushed himself, and in the process learned he could do something he didn't necessarily want to or even expect he could do. He didn't win. In week seven of the competition, he was voted off. Nonetheless, up until that very last dance, he performed with skill and dignity, prompting the show's longtime cohost Tom Bergeron to say he was "leaving on a night when he excelled."

After doing *Dancing with the Stars*, Hayes relocated to Los Angeles. He signed with a major Hollywood talent agency and made a deal to appear in *Freakish*, a horror series for Hulu with YouTubers Meghan Rienks and Liza Koshy, about high school students who come head-to-head with a bunch of mutants.

As soon as Hayes began *Dancing with the Stars*, he needed to be out on the West Coast. Nash had already been living in L.A. for about two years when the next thing he knew, his little brother had claimed his couch as home. Soon Hayes moved into a nice place with a bunch of roommates, which was a lot of freedom for a fifteen-year-old.

The whole situation perplexed Nash, because when he moved out west, he had a twenty-four-hour bodyguard and needed to call his dad every morning at eight o'clock.

I was on lockdown.

But their parents apparently didn't think the same level of supervision was necessary when it came to Hayes. Maybe it was because Nash was already out here, and they had seen their middle son figure out how to manage on his own.

The situation was very much to Hayes's liking, but Nash didn't know if so much independence was ultimately going to be good or bad for his little brother. Hayes definitely needed a reality check when he first moved to L.A.

> He will do whatever's in front of him. You have no idea how crazy that kid is. Trust me. You can't measure the things he has done in order of stupidity. For example, he bought a car—and he doesn't have a license. He can't even drive!

Hayes was very much still a kid, but living in a very adult situation. As a teenager, he thought he knew everything, even though he still had a lot to figure out. Hayes had a lot of talent, and a lot of potential. He just didn't know what he wanted to do with any of it. Nash was so anxious to see how things turned out for him, in no small part because he felt personally responsible for the situation his little brother was in.

> All three of us—Will, Hayes, and I—we've been through a lot. But each of us has come through our moments of adversity. Hayes, who is very smart, grew up fast, in a good way, and is now mature beyond his years.

Because the life in the public eye Nash chose for himself instantly became Hayes's, Nash was compelled to continue to shape his little brother's decisions. He had to steer him toward the right path, tell him to stay on top of his schoolwork, and other stuff Hayes really didn't want to hear. Nash turned into dad mode in order to keep Hayes in line whenever he could. When Hayes was around, Nash instantly turned into an old person—not because he enjoyed it.

Nash didn't come out to L.A. to be his brother's babysitter. He had his own life, his own adventures, and his own friends—including Justin Bieber. The superfamous singer, the guy who almost blew up Twitter after he created an account, reached out to Nash not long after he had moved to L.A. to invite him to a rooftop party.

> That was honestly one of the best parties I've ever been to. There were all these extremely cool people there, actors, musicians, professional athletes—just the most random, famous people were hanging out around the bar and hot tub. Insanely famous people. I specifically remember being blown away that Dave Chappelle was there. But because it was a rooftop, the party was also kind of small and intimate, so it was really easy to have conversations. I spent the entire night talking and listening to all these amazing people, learning what they were about and being really inspired. It was the whole reason I came out to L.A. embodied in one night out on the town.

The first time Nash met J.B., the recording artist was taking a break from making new music and touring—the first break in the seven years since he had broken out on the scene at age twelve. It was clearly a tough period for him, which some called his "negative phase." During this hiatus, he was just as relevant as he's always been, but he needed to take some time for himself.

J.B. came out of that phase with so much wisdom and knowledge, which Nash uses as an example for his own life. Like Nash, J.B. got his start on social media. He was discovered by a talent manager through his YouTube videos, in which he covered pop hits. By the time Nash got to know the performer, he had already successfully done everything Nash could ever imagine doing and more.

Nash never planned on becoming a pop star, but he admired the way J.B. took over so many industries. There are the obvious ones he's dominated, like fashion and fragrance. And of course, he's a leader on social media. On Twitter alone, he has more than 82 million followers. Less well known, however, is his widespread, active investing into private tech start-ups. J.B. has put millions into social media platforms, gaming companies, and other things he's interested in. He was an early backer of Spotify, when nobody even knew what that was. The fact that one person could make that big an impact on the world was very inspiring to Nash.

J.B. dropped a lot of big-brother-type stuff on me. Some of it had to do with the business and the things he's learned over the years. But mostly, he's given me advice on how to focus on what actually matters when you're out in L.A. J.B.'s advice to me was that in order to make people happy—which ultimately is what both of us want to do— you have to make sure you are happy, too. Real happiness doesn't come from any outside material source. You can't buy it, or find it in some object. In order to access that true, raw happiness, you sometimes have to change your mind-set, friends, and surroundings. The soul-searching it requires is not easy, but it's crucial. When you are happy, that's when you're operating at your full potential. That's when you can fully do what it is that you were born to do, fulfill that which is your purpose.

Nash and Justin don't spend all their time together having heart-to-hearts. Usually they're too busy doing cool stuff that J.B.'s hooked them up with—like sitting courtside at a Clippers game or chilling poolside at his pad. J.B.'s invited Nash into so many amazing experiences, but above all motivated him to grow/ learn in ways Nash couldn't have imagined.

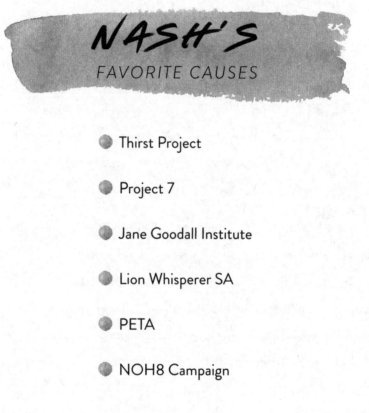

NASH'S
FAVORITE CAUSES

- Thirst Project

- Project 7

- Jane Goodall Institute

- Lion Whisperer SA

- PETA

- NOH8 Campaign

CHAPTER 14

Nash returned home to North Carolina for a week in 2016 to get away from the distractions of Los Angeles. Not that home doesn't have its own distractions. He spent the first couple of days just hanging out with his family and catching up, getting up to speed on all those little details that you can't get any other way than by being face-to-face.

Returning home is so nice and easy. I need that vibe every now and then. Having a huge family to be around has really come in clutch.

This trip was especially meaningful, because his mom, Johnnie, and Skylynn were about to move to a farm. Everything in the house on Lake Norman that Nash grew up in was almost all boxed up. As they dealt with the last details of moving to their new home, which Hayes and Nash put money toward pur-

NOTHING BETTER THAN BEING BAREFOOT OUTSIDE

chasing, the boys realized that this was a marker of what they'd achieved so far. The gorgeous land on the property became symbolic of that.

Most people knew that Hayes and Nash were brothers, since their audiences were intertwined. But sometimes folks were amazed when they found out that Will Grier is their older brother. As one of the top high school recruits, he became the starting quarterback at the University of Florida, part of the Southeastern Conference, the most prestigious division in college football. Will was ranked one of the nation's top twenty quarterbacks. He didn't let games with stadiums of 100,000 fans slow him down. As a freshman playing for the Gators, he burst out onto the scene with a string of dramatic victories. He was being hailed as the next Tim Tebow. But just as quickly as he rose, Nash's big brother came crashing down.

The day after a 21–3 victory against Missouri, Will learned from his coach that he had tested positive for a performance-enhancing drug and would be suspended from playing for a year. He couldn't believe it. To bulk up, the young quarterback had been using protein powder that he bought from a nutrition supplement store in Gainesville. Someone who worked there suggested Will try Ligandrol, a supplement to gain muscle mass. Although that specific make of the drug was not on the NCAA's list of banned substances, the type of drug, a selective androgen receptor modulator, *is* prohibited by the national organization. Will thought he'd covered his bases when he checked on the internet to make sure Ligandrol passed NCAA regulations. But he should have run it by Florida's trainers. He wasn't cheating; he had just made a mistake.

It was hard for Nash to watch his brother's press conference the day after he got the bad news. Will fought tears as he apologized to his team and the world for his mistake and expressed his hope that he would learn something from it.

I bawled my eyes out watching his press conference. The guy I look up to for everything and he's crushed. I thought he couldn't come back from that.

Thankfully Will did come back from it, although the road back was rough. Like Nash, Will came to understand that when you are in the spotlight, any mistake you make is a big one. And you have to fight to come back from it.

First, Will went through a dark period after his suspension, when he felt shunned by his team and coach in Florida. Usually an optimistic person, he would sit up at night, brooding about the events of the past year. Who was he if he wasn't a quarterback? Will's whole identity was wrapped up in football, and now he worried he'd lost it all because of some advice he took from a guy at a nutrition and supplement store.

Luckily, he had Jeanne to help him through. Will had met his future wife not long after he arrived in Gainesville, and the two instantly clicked. A former Buccaneers cheerleader, Jeanne understood the pressure-cooker world of football and, more important, loved Will. Nash's older brother also returned home to Charlotte and Davidson Day for a little while. There, in the place where he honed the talents that took him to a superstar level, he had a chance to regroup and redevelop. He joined his dad at the Davidson Day games as an analyst, a role that helped remind him why he played this game in the first place. Because he loved it.

Nash's older brother ended up playing at West Virginia University, where the coach believed in Will as a person—so much so that he promised him a scholarship no matter how long the NCAA decided to keep him out of the game. That meant a lot to the quarterback, who also became a dad in November 2016, when, Eloise, his and Jeanne's daughter, was born. So was Will trying to not only move past his very public humiliation but also deal with a new school, new football team, and new baby! But Chad Grier's sons do not give up, and Will fought through.

He battled through not playing for two straight years.

In the fall of 2017 he was finally back on the football field. As the Mountaineers quarterback that season, he passed for 3,490 yards and 34 touchdowns—even though he broke a finger on his throwing hand! Because of his miraculous performance—and long brown hair—Mountaineer fans starting calling Will "Touchdown Jesus."

Will decided to return to West Virginia for another season, a fifth-year senior, instead of entering the 2018 NFL draft. Throughout Will's entire college career in Morgantown, Chad never missed a Mountaineers game—not one—even though he lived almost six hundred miles from the WVU campus. By this point, Chad had left his position at Davidson Day to become the head coach at Oceanside Collegiate Academy near Charleston, South Carolina. Although the charter school had never won a football game before (to be fair, the school was only two years old), after Chad took over the team had a record of 7–3, leading the school to promote him to athletics director.

Despite his new responsibilities at work, Chad often made the nine-hour drive through the night in order to make it to Morgantown before the game started, so he could see Will. It was a little—or a lot—harder when Chad had to travel to away games in places like Texas, which required air travel. He didn't get home from the Oceanside football games he coached until one in the morning early Saturday morning. Finding a commercial flight that would get him to Will's games by kickoff on Saturday was impossible. Luckily, a family friend who lives back in Charlotte had a private plane he let Chad use so that he never had to miss a single one of his son's games.

Thanks to the support of his entire family and his refusal to give up, Will entered into the 2019 NFL draft as one of its top picks. Nash is really happy for him, although he does worry about his big brother—especially when he sees some of the hits Will takes on the field. At the level of play he's in, everyone on that field pretty much defies physics. There are six-foot-five, 290-pound linemen who run 40-yard dashes in four seconds. When you take a couple of hits from these guys—whose goal is to tackle you as hard as they can—it can really be damaging not only in the short term, but also in the long term. Will, who's had his fair share of crazy injuries, told Nash about how some games he would end up getting sacked multiple times, and that the difference between taking four major hits to the ground versus five is life-changing.

"You're not just going to stop," Will said. "You've worked your entire life to get there—even if you're blacking out, whatever it is, you're not going to stop."

Nash worried about his big brother but he understood the relentless drive toward the pursuit of his goals. That was something all three of them—Will, Nash, and Hayes—had in common. And they were being rewarded for it. There was one point where Will was playing for Florida on national TV pretty much every week, Hayes was on *Dancing with the Stars,* and Nash had just started to do the press tour for *The Outfield.*

They were rewarded for their hard work in many ways.

Just as Dad always said, "Hard work works."

And one of the rewards was the farm in North Carolina, where Skylynn can grow up with animals, and their mom can grow her own food. Not to mention become an influencer herself.

Elizabeth followed in her sons' footsteps and started to make her own online content—albeit for a very different audience than that of Nash and Hayes. "Digital media matriarch Elizabeth Grier-Floyd has launched her very own southern lifestyle channel on YouTube," Tubefilter announced when the channel went live

ME AND MY GIRLS IN NORTH CAROLINA

in 2016. Moms are fans of Elizabeth's videos on cooking, design, fashion, and family. But as Elizabeth put it, "I'm not a fashionista, interior designer, or actress, just superpassionate about sharing our gifts and souls with each other!"

As a mom of four who has experienced her fair share of ups and downs, Elizabeth wanted to offer some of the wisdom she picked up along "this journey called life." There's no topic off limits as she makes vegan corn salsa with Skylynn, takes viewers on a tour of her farmhouse, shows the yoga moves to get her biceps, or shares intimate revelations on how she coped with the death of her father when she was young and later her divorce from Chad. People have responded to her authenticity just as they have with her sons'. Her Instagram account, @therealelizabethgrierfloyd, has 335,000 followers! Not bad for a "farm livin, DIYer, yoga worshipper and cooking addict!" And grandma!

It's always hard for Nash to leave Skylynn and his mom, but after his weeklong visit in 2016 he was off to Charlotte to meet up with his friends flying in from L.A. and then to pick up his merch for a meet and greet. They were going to carpool all the way down to Myrtle Beach, South Carolina, where Nash hadn't been since he was a kid. There, they were going to do a meet and greet and an hourlong stage performance at the county fair, which tens of thousands of people attend. Then Nash was set to fly out to Los Angeles, where he was due on set the next day for *You Get Me*, an updated, younger *Fatal Attraction* starring Bella Thorne. The shoot for the film went through the first week of May—the same week Nash also started rehearsals for

FIRST DAY ON THE SET OF <u>YOU GET ME</u> WITH BELLA THORNE
AND TAYLOR JOHN SMITH

his Latin American tour, The Wave, which was scheduled to kick off May 9.

Nash named the tour The Wave because all the guys on it—Rudy Mancuso, DJ Rupp, Alec Bailey, and Tez Mengestu—were part of the next wave of people Nash believed would actually make an impact and change the world.

Ever since I did my first meet-and-greet convention, live events in this internet space have been that you just meet people. That's cool, but I wanted to do a real show. So with The Wave, I produced an actual show with lights, music, a DJ, emcee, and skits. We still have the meet-and-greet portion, but we also put on a damn good show.

Ever since his improv days, Nash has always admired theater—the raw experience of a roomful of people, who aren't eating, drinking, or talking. They're just laser-focused while the actors deliver emotions.

Live humans are the screen.

That's what he was really excited about doing during his tour, which would take him through Latin America: Santiago, Chile; Rio de Janeiro, Brazil; Buenos Aires, Argentina; Lima, Peru; and Mexico City.

FIRST SHOW IN ARGENTINA DURING THE WAVE TOUR IN 2017

Throughout this whole period—whether hanging out with his mom and Skylynn or rocking it in Rio—Nash was still making his videos, which he tried to post every Sunday, and getting at least a piece of content on each one of his platforms.

How do I share a piece of myself, interact with others, do a call to action? These questions are never far from my mind, no matter what else is going on in my life. That's because I know that the people on the other end of my posts, tweets, Snapchats, and videos are the essence of my success.

Nash DMs pretty much all his fans, and he follows more than 58,000 of them and counting. That's what keeps it all going.

PLANNING THE WAVE, MY FIRST INTERNATIONAL TOUR

Retweeting, reposting. If he reposts something a fan writes and shows what they say to his millions of followers, that in turn gets them thousands of retweets or posts. That's the excitement and why a pretty good chunk of his fans are with him forever.

It takes time, following more than 58,000 people. It's definitely not easy interacting and communicating on such a wide scale on a daily basis while also trying to push out his own messages and inspiration. Nash spends a lot of time on it every day, just on social media. It's usually the first thing he does. But one of the most important things for him is that others can get their words to him just as easily as he can get his word to anyone else.

I'm very accessible. I can hear and see anything; all you have to do is tag me in a tweet.

If Nash was not a people person, it would be hard being so accessible. And he wasn't always a people person. This journey has made him one. Ever since his first meet and greets in Dallas, Orlando, and D.C., and his meet-up in Iceland, he learned how to get in tune with what people have to say and offer. Because Nash reached out by posting a video or a tweet, it was easier to talk to him. Although he didn't realize it initially, he was starting a conversation.

I was starting a movement: <u>I'm talking to you, to each one of you.</u>

Nash's followers feel that. In return, he gets to feel their ecstatic responses and their high expectations, which push him to always be better.

Every single person who comes through, whatever they're doing, whatever they want, Nash makes sure to mirror it, so that they are satisfied by the interaction.

But obviously, only if what a person is putting out is positive.

It's not a technique or strategy he employs. It's just something that happens naturally. As soon as a person walks into a meet and greet, Nash looks him or her in the eyes and gives them a hug.

I'm big on the hugs. I'm just a hugging guy. I feel like a hug is medicine for the soul.

If you're buying a ticket to come to a show or for a meet and greet, or whatever it is, you already have your expectations and what you want to get when you buy that ticket. That's already in your head. By the time you get there, why would Nash give you anything different than what you expect?

He hugs and sits with his fans. He talks to them. Whatever they want, they get. What his fans want, though, is all over the place.

"Can I get a video for my friend? She couldn't make it."

"Can I get a hug?"

"Can you carry me on your back?"

"Can we take this picture?"

"Can we do this pose?"

Nash really never has to say no to any request. He does a bunch of weird stuff, like poses for pictures you wouldn't expect. A lot of times it's more of an I-love-you-so-much-let-me-just-tackle-you kind of thing, which he's also made acceptable at his meet and greets and in public.

I'm not above anything. In fact, I'm all for it. You're here with your expectations. I'm here to fulfill them. That's how it should always be. I hate people who use their fans by taking the numbers they bring and the power that comes with it, then skipping out when their followers ask something of them. Smiling for a photo, then moving on to the next person is not intimate and not okay.

There's an actual relationship between Nash and his fans, the people who follow him. He has a real connection with them and a real respect for them. For the past four years, they have developed an understanding, as they learn and grow together. To see more and more people join this audience has been beautiful for Nash to witness, because what they are doing is spreading messages of love.

If Nash can give kids—who maybe aren't so sure about what they're doing with their lives, or what's going on with the entire world—a little bit of sanity and clarity that they might not have had before, simply by sharing their stories, then he's done something good. Nash's story turns into a bunch of stories about trying to explain what can't be easily explained but should at least be tried.

My goal is to make everyone realize that they have a purpose and a true meaning—and that they're not only wanted, but they're needed on earth to make a difference and to make a change.

That's why every single thing Nash posts is dear to his heart. Every quote or retweet means something to him. He's not just tossing stuff out there, but building a movement one post at a time. He's making content on all different platforms to access and interact with people who need a little bit of happiness, advice, or motivation.

These are messages that aren't necessarily being promoted widely. Nash doesn't like to take sides, or pick labels, or do any of that stuff. He likes to look at every perspective. His ultimate goal is to unearth what's buried inside humans and close to our hearts, because these are the things that need to be talked about the most.

If I have a purpose, this is it: through my experiences, to guide people on how to thrive. How can you live your life to the fullest? Not just experience it, but also affect other people positively?

Nash has no idea how far this experiment can go, but it's been going pretty far. Millions of people have followed his journey, and he's followed tens of thousands of people's journeys on Twitter, and more on Instagram and other social media platforms. Some of his fan accounts have been around for years, and have hundreds of thousands of followers of their own.

I'm not the only source for these accounts. Instead, we are like ecosystems within one another.

The content is pure love and passion. And just like those two emotions, it's also free to use as you wish. People take Nash's content and remake it all the time. Sometimes they riff on a post or go as far as to edit his videos into something that's new and wholly theirs. It's an ongoing cycle. Nash gives stuff to others, and they give it back to him. What he's learned is that the harder he pushes on this wheel, the more powerfully it returns to him. So he strives to spin it as fast as he can. He wants to make people aware of every issue and every tool available, from a perspective of hope.

Some of the coolest things he's done in his career have been the most interactive. One of them is called #FacetimeMeNash, which he begins by telling his followers to tweet the hashtag in order to get it trending. Then he goes through those who have retweeted it and picks random people with whom to FaceTime. The amazing thing is that he gets people who respond from all over the world. He's had folks reach out from South Africa, Egypt, New Zealand, Indonesia, and Ethiopia! Those are just a few of the countries, but it's all over. There's almost nowhere on this planet that the internet's power can't reach—except for those places with authoritarian regimes. Even in those countries, though, young people often find ways around the repression.

In order to celebrate that, and because Nash is fascinated with learning more about international perspectives that are new

#FACETIMEMENASH-ING WITH FANS

to him, he tries to pick different people from all over the world
when he does #FacetimeMeNash. It doesn't matter if they're in
Italy or Ecuador: he connects with them face-to-face to hear
and see what's going on in their lives. He can basically do everything he does in a meet and greet, other than give them a hug.
It's such a great collaboration with his followers that every time
he announces the hashtag, it goes to number one on Twitter
instantly.

People love it, because it's all about connection.

Despite its huge popularity on Twitter, Nash wanted even
more people to know about #FacetimeMeNash. It wasn't just that
his fans were so into it. *He* was so into it! Every time he traveled

across the globe through his phone, he dove into a new culture and learned and experienced so much. So Nash decided to make a short film about it. He went on his computer one morning and sat there all day, FaceTiming people while he filmed their conversations. From an entire day of conversations with people all over the world, he cut a twenty-minute video, which he posted. In it, he gave courage to a girl in England getting an operation, met kids' moms and dads, and told people how awesome they are. There was a lot of emotion—a girl from Italy broke down in tears. There was a light side too, as people talked about whom they would hang out with if they could hang out with anyone, living, dead, or cartoon. A grandma in Brazil brought down some serious wisdom when she called for the union of everyone in the world under the banner of tolerance. Perhaps most important, Nash got to thank everyone—face-to-face—for their support.

Having that direct feedback from real people is important to him. He needs to know what's happening out in the world as much as anyone else.

I don't want any kind of filter between my followers and me.

Nash thinks filters are just bad, which is why he finds the internet a good place to be. Anything you want to know about is at your fingertips. If you see something trending, just click it and scroll, and in twenty minutes of scanning and reading you can be caught up on an issue or event—from politics to culture or science—not just from one side but from many, many perspectives.

*I'm not naïve. I know probably better than a
lot of others that there are many lies on the
internet—more than there are truths.*

Crowdsourcing a topic allows for a rounded picture of any subject, and it's easy to do when there are as many people weighing in as there are on Twitter's trending topics.

In addition to articles from reputable sources, Twitter allows you to read raw opinions. They are short bursts of thought in 280 characters, but you have so many of them that you get every single angle under the sun. It's not just one person, one voice, or one company controlling the narrative. Read fifty, one hundred, two hundred of these, plus pictures and videos, and then a few articles, and from all these sources you can put together your own opinions and thoughts on whatever subject you're researching.

Since you can go direct to the source of any story, why wouldn't you? Why would you have anyone filter anything for you? Social media is great for debate and opinion. But when you want to head to meatier subjects, like global warming or the history of religion, you are obviously going to have to read stuff that's a little longer than 280 characters. But again, Nash challenges people to create their own investigation by combing search engines for experts, thought leaders, and others passionate about whatever subject they're looking into. They can then assess the validity of the experts they find by researching their credentials. Is someone an actual scientist or just spouting opinion? Do sources devote themselves to studying a subject, writing books, and teaching—or are they getting paid by a corporation to put out whatever they're saying? There are ways to find out all of these things and more.

Ironically, the internet—or more specifically social media—is one of the greatest sources of disinformation and division. That's why there is no excuse for not educating yourself and taking control of the information you consume. You have to go in deep; you have to dig; you have to read; you have to watch. Most important, you have to challenge your own biases. If you think you know something, Nash encourages you to look at it from the other sides—good, bad, or anything in the middle. What's the alternative? Endless conflict between rigid beliefs.

Questioning your opinion and thinking in a new way, seen through other people's minds, is not easy.

That's something I have worked really, really, really hard on. I continue to work on how to see things from other perspectives. My dream is to see from as many different perspectives as possible, including the poorest, most uneducated individual all the way to a titan of industry and thought like Elon Musk. How can I get everyone's views, so that when I'm asked something, or find myself in a situation where I need to take action, I don't react by instinct, but instead react by thought? That's the only way, I believe, to truly better the situation we are in.

In this time in the world, we have more information than ever but seem more fractured than ever. Nash takes solace in the fact that when you explore many diverging points of view on one subject, you sometimes find a beautiful unity. That's what he found with religion.

What's more divisive than religion? It is still the main reason for many wars, violence, and personal pain. Nash believes that there is a Creator. But he also believes that some people use their specific religion as a title and a label, not all that different than the citizenship of a country or a professional title.

I really hate labels. I see so many religious people who aren't actually religious, meaning they aren't in their religion for the actual connection of it—to God, nature, fellow man, or themselves. Instead, they are just in it for themselves.

Nash grew up Christian. At the end of the day, he believes it's good to be in touch with everything that's going on in the religious world. It's interesting for him to learn about the pope and the Jewish people, Buddhists and Muslims, too. It's amazing to him that there are millions of people who are all dead set on their different religions—and all in the same rigid way.

Nash has done a lot of reflecting on the subject of religion. Reading a lot of books where science and religion meet opened up many questions for him.

What is the right story?

Where does my belief go?

Most religions have the same overall kind of story—not the exact same story, but similar archetypes, prophets, and messages. It might seem contradictory, but there is something in the collective nature of belief that makes Nash think religion should ultimately be a personal endeavor.

> I think everyone should have his or her own connection with God—and should be given the space to figure it out. Every religion has value and the power to change how you look at life, but faith is not something you can get from another person. You don't need a human to tell you about your faith.

Obviously, no one's lived to tell what happens after death. In terms of the afterlife, what do heaven and hell even mean? How can anyone tell anyone else what heaven or hell is?

> My heaven can be very different from your heaven. My hell can be very different from your hell. The only way that I'm going to be able to determine heaven and hell is if I live my entire life to know: what's the worst; what's the best; what's good; what's bad; what's evil; what's peace; what's love?

All of us have a purpose. I really believe that.

Nash also believes people can live their whole lives trying to find that purpose and never succeed. Even worse, though, are the people who don't even try. They don't recognize their connection to the divine and to the rest of humanity.

That, to me, is the saddest thing.

All of this goes back to a question of perspective—basically, your mind and the power that it has on your life. You can do pretty much anything you want; you can change the way your world works, based solely on your thoughts. We're all a living representation of our thoughts.

In thinking about these huge existential questions about the nature of the universe and our place as humans in it, Nash believes you have to look at everything from both a scientific and spiritual perspective. There are things that just can't be explained fully with only one or the other. Whether it's God, science, or some force that combines the two that we can never fully comprehend, there exists the ultimate connection.

There is that expression of "life flashing before your eyes." Nash had instances where he was almost hit by a car or was in a car that was almost hit—and he experienced the feeling of that flash. It's like an instinct. Humans are programmed to try their hardest to remember the things most important to them, most special, when they're about to die or think they are. That's something we've evolved to do.

This might sound weird, but I have an image of myself right before I die. Hopefully it won't be for a very, very long time, but I wonder what will fill my "flash." I know one thing for certain—whenever it happens, I will still be telling stories.

Around the time Nash got his first hundred thousand followers on Vine, he started to explore his purpose on this earth. It wasn't about Vine—or social media, or even the internet. It was about connection. Storytelling. It doesn't matter if it's a video, tweet, documentary, Snapchat, IG post, meet and greet, or full-length feature.

I find meaning in any kind of narrative that fosters connection.

Ever since those early days on social media, Nash has been trying to develop his purpose into the biggest scale possible. In the beginning, when he wasn't sure if the huge response he was getting online was just a fluke, anything more than his fifteen minutes of fame, he was driven to continue doing what he was doing by the thought *What if I could just change one person's life?*

That question turned into "What if I can change a hundred people's lives?" Then, "What if I could change a thousand lives?" Until he arrived at "What if we can start a movement?"

CHAPTER 15

Nash changed many times over since moving to L.A. "Every month feels like a year," he says as he reflects on his most recent travels. In 2018 Nash achieved a lifelong goal of traveling to Africa, not once but twice.

His mission—to help end the suffering of those who don't have clean drinking water—started far, far away . . . in the excess and glamor of Italy's fashion week. That year, Nash was walking in Dolce & Gabbana's show. It wasn't his first time walking the runway for the Italian luxury brand known for its brazen styles (Madonna is a huge fan). He had already been in one show where by mistake one of his outfits had leather, which, like fur, Nash doesn't wear. Not wearing any type of animal was a stipulation to him walking in the show. Nash ended up wearing the leather, because he is a professional and didn't want to ruin the show. But that was the last time the designers made that mistake.

WITH CAM BACKSTAGE AT THE DOLCE & GABBANA
FASHION SHOW IN 2018

It was also one of the last few times Nash saw Cameron Dallas, who was also walking in the Dolce & Gabbana show. The
differences between the two came years earlier, when Cam took
over and revived MagCon, which had been struggling.

*That was the dagger point. We talked about it every
day for a week and I kept telling him how stupid
I thought it was to take it over.*

It wasn't a stupid business decision at all. In fact, it probably was a great one in terms of profits. But it was a decision based on a very different value system than the one Nash was developing for himself. In Nash's eyes, he was trying to grow up, parlay the fame he'd been given as a young person into something more meaningful and lasting rather than just another moneymaking opportunity. To him, MagCon represented reliving the past—and not in a good way.

Nash and Cam were in very different places by 2016. Nash was trying to find his place and purpose on this earth. He was putting his personal growth first exploring religion, politics, movies.

I watched every single David Lynch film and then read all about him. . . . Did you know the film director has been practicing meditation seriously since 1973, so seriously he set up a foundation to promote it?

Nash felt like he was learning and growing a lot even if he wasn't making millions for his agents. Even his diet was part of this evolution. He had become vegan, meaning he doesn't eat any animal products, including cheese, eggs, and honey. Being vegan gives him a sense of ownership over his own life. Plus, it makes him feel great.

I have a lot of energy. Except when I went to South America. I lost fifteen pounds in ten days in those heavy meat-eating countries, where I basically lived off avocados. Being vegan in Jamaica, Bali, and Africa is much easier.

Meanwhile, Cam was riding the newest wave of social media, which at that time was musical.ly—an app that allowed people to make short lip-synching videos customized by using different filters, effects, and speeds. "Musers" were so young (often twelve and younger) that they made Nash and his crew seem old as the hills. And they were growing. In June 2016, the app registered more than 90 million users, which by the end of May 2017 had grown to over 200 million. Cam didn't let a few years get in the way of him becoming one of them and blowing up again by gaining a huge new, young audience. Nash wasn't interested in musical.ly.

I was trying to have a voice that meant something and I saw musical.ly as a threat to that.

By the time the two old friends saw each other in Italy for their second Dolce & Gabbana show, Nash and Cam had become more like strangers. Their brands were once one and the same as they rose up together to become two of the world's biggest influencers. And then they were out of touch with each other. Nash mourned the loss of the close friendship. He didn't think Cam was a bad person or wished him any ill will.

For two years we had gone through the same thing, been to the same parties, dealt with the same problems. You can't have hard feelings when those days end. It was a great relationship.

But Nash wasn't interested in making money off of other people's success, which was the business model at the time for MagCon, no matter how profitable.

I don't know what was smarter, but I'm still glad I did what I did. I never wanted that.

All industries change, whether it's auto manufacturing or media.

First Blockbuster, now Toys"R"Us. 😦 STAY WOKE, CHUCK E. CHEESE'S!

But perhaps no business in history has changed faster than social media. Maybe that's because the technology itself is so quickly consumed. Nash became a superstar practically overnight thanks to Vine, the app that took off in 2012. But only four years after purchasing that mobile video-sharing service for $30 million, Twitter shut it down. "Thank you. Thank you. To all the creators out there—thank you for taking a chance on this app back in the day," Twitter said in its October 2016 announcement that it was ending Vine. "Thank you to all of those who came to watch and laugh every day."

Unfortunately, with the rise of so many other different social media platforms, not enough people were watching to keep Vine alive. Snapchat and even musical.ly, with their improved capabilities, had taken a big bite out of Vine's users and audience. While Nash stayed away from musical.ly, he didn't give up on social media once Vine was no more. Like a lot of other influencers, he had big followings on Instagram and Twitter. Although he had a YouTube account since 2012, Nash didn't really start posting new material on it until 2017. Still, he quickly gained a huge audience of 4.8 million subscribers with over 80 million views!

So when Nash was locked out of his YouTube account in October 2017 after he disabled his own access by mistake, there were a lot of upset fans. "Got locked out of my YT account. I'll have videos up as soon as I'm back in," Nash tweeted. Two hours later he tweeted again, crowdsourcing the question "Should I just post the videos directly to Twitter or wait for YouTube support?" YouTube replied back to Nash on Twitter, saying, "Our Creator Support team is reaching out for further help, hope this gets resolved soon!"

Nash didn't hold it against YouTube, but he's also not devoted to the platform for his video content, either. Nash is open to any platform where he can get his message across. Two days after Instagram launched IGTV, Nash posted his first video to that service, which streams long-form vertically oriented video. Although IGTV didn't take off like other apps, Nash continued to post a new IGTV video almost every Sunday because he found it visually exciting to play with the vertical format. He put up a post on August 26, 2018, of his adventures in Dubai, which only got 36,680 views. That might sound like a lot. Considering Nash has 9.9 million followers on Instagram, however, it's not exactly a big response. Looking at vibrant colors of the varied spices in a market, the wide expanse of golden sand of the Arabian Desert, or Nash's bright blue eyes from beneath a kaffiyeh, it's clear that the medium held some artistic inspiration for him.

Nash's efforts—whether online or in real life—have never been just about numbers. He doesn't do things for self-promotion. That's definitely not why he went on an influencers' trip to Africa in March 2018, after the Dolce & Gabbana fashion show in Italy.

Nash had been wanting to go there for a long time and finally got the chance when the filmmaker and YouTuber FunforLouis organized a trip to experience South Africa.

Louis John Cole—aka FunforLouis or, as Nash said, the "Grandfather of YouTube"—is a DJ who began vlogging when he took a road trip on a double-decker bus around his native England in 2012. That was just the start of a career of turning adventures in meeting new people and visiting new places, extremely far-flung or hidden closer to home, into video content that he hopes will motivate his more than two million followers on YouTube to seek out their own adventures. That's the inspiration for the catchphrase he often ends his clips with: "How will you live your adventure?"

Louis billed the weeklong trip to South Africa that Nash and Taylor joined that March as "Live the Adventure." Nash was among ten top influencers who had agreed to explore the country, which has vast and varied natural ecosystems, diverse and deep cultures, and plenty of wildlife. Another social media star included was Zack Kalter. A former professional baseball player, he had gained fame as a contestant on the ninth season of *The Bachelorette* and then later on *Bachelor in Paradise*. Also on hand was Zack's girlfriend and Instagram model Helen Owen, who had a little over a million people following her trips around the world, where she explored her love of food and design. There were other travel influencers, like Chelsea Yamase, a Hawaii-based blogger who tries to inspire her followers "to view the world as precious and connected rather than fierce or unfamiliar." And the Polish-born Aggie Lal, who boasts on her website, Travelinhershoes.com, that's she's visited fifty-three countries!

Louis packed in the activities for this group of professional travelers, who kayaked with dolphins, enjoyed the surf with penguins, chilled with lots of animals while on safari, flew in helicopters, took road trips, and hung out in the pool of one of Cape Town's most luxurious villas.

Nash enjoyed everything the trip had to offer, including a new friendship with one of the behind-the-scenes organizers, Kyle Mijlof.

I connected to him more than anyone else. He's a very enlightened being.

Kyle took Nash to places not typically visited by tourists so that the American could experience, even if only briefly, normal life and people in the area.

It wasn't just the fact that Kyle was born and raised in Cape Town that made him a great tour guide. He's also an expert traveler. His personal journey began in 2010 after he graduated from college with a degree in sound design and a plan to work in movies. Instead, he picked up a camera and flew to Morocco to spend the next six months exploring western Africa, taking pictures in such countries as Mauritania, Senegal, Mali, Ghana, Togo, Benin, Nigeria, Namibia, and more before returning to South Africa.

Bit by the wandering bug, Kyle then decided to do the same thing along the east coast of Africa. Since he first took off, he's been to seventy countries, including New Zealand, Fiji, and Indonesia.

Kyle's journeys have not always been easy. Far from it. On that first trip, he got malaria four times within five months (twice in Ghana, once in Cameroon, and lastly while camping in the Democratic Republic of Congo, where he was so delirious from fever that he started talking to a tree). He narrowly escaped major conflicts on several of his trips, missing the uprising in Egypt's Tahrir Square by a couple of weeks and leaving Syria a month before civil war broke out. He was forced out of Mali when the Tuareg rebellion began. But nothing stops him. Kyle rode a scooter through more than a thousand miles of desert, and in India he did a six-day, nearly 700-mile rickshaw run from Goa to Mumbai.

Through Kyle, Nash learned about "Day Zero," the term Cape Town was using for the day the city's taps run dry, forcing people to line up for water. Predictions originally put the catastrophic day in August 2018, but because of massive water conservation efforts on the part of the city's residents, they averted drought—

at least until the following year. Nash was astounded by the South African urbanites, who cut their water consumption by more than 50 percent, living on no more than 13 gallons per person a day. It was a shock to come from the United States to a place where you flush the toilet judiciously, take very short showers, and clean your hands with sanitizer. Even in top hotels, there are buckets to collect the water to be used again. It was also inspiring.

The introduction Kyle offered him to regular life in Africa, at least in the small corner that he visited, was enough to make Nash want to return and do something to help the continent, which has a history of being colonized and plundered by the rest of the world. He just had no idea how quickly he would be back.

A couple of months after first traveling to Africa, Nash returned, this time to Swaziland (now known as Eswatini). His mission was to bring clean drinking water to people in great need. The 1.1 million people of this small landlocked country, which borders South Africa, were in need of a lot. According to UNICEF, Swaziland has the highest rate of HIV infection of any country in the world. Not only are hundreds of thousands of its citizens living with the virus, but it has also taken many lives and left many orphans behind. But Nash wanted to focus on drinking water since he was already a supporter of the Thirst Project, a youth water activist group.

Thirst Project, which was begun in 2008 by seven nineteen-year-old friends in Southern California, has a mission to "build a socially-conscious generation of young people who end the global water crisis." One in every eight humans, or one billion people on earth, don't have access to safe drinking water. According to the group, the problems of clean water and sanitation are the number-one global killer of children. "Waterborne diseases kill more children every single year than AIDS, malaria, and all world violence combined," the group's site claims. Eight percent of all global diseases are waterborne, killing 4,100 children every day. More than 2.2 million people die every year from something they caught drinking water!

The Thirst Project—which raised over $8 million to fund projects that have brought clean water to more than 280,000 people—set its sights on Swaziland and bringing clean water and sanitation to the *entire country* by 2022. "By providing a community with safe drinking water, disease rates can drop by up to 88% virtually overnight!" the group argues. "Child mortality rates can drop up to 90%—overnight! Clean water also plays an incredibly critical role in effectively treating and managing HIV/AIDS in rural communities." This is crucial in Swaziland, where even if its citizens have access to medication, if they have to drink contaminated water with compromised immune systems, the outcome can easily be fatal.

The year before this trip, Nash had asked that fans donate to the organization for his birthday, eventually raising around $13,000 to build wells in Africa. He was heartbroken to hear about conditions in the impoverished country where women and children spend on average six to eight hours a day walking to get water. "Women and children walk crazy distances, sometimes over four miles, just to get contaminated water," Nash explained to his followers about his reason for raising money. "You have to drink water to survive."

Spending time in Swaziland building wells was, as Nash put it, "a life-changing experience." With Taylor and Kyle by his side, he watched three-year-olds carrying buckets of diseased water for miles. The process of getting water takes so long for many children every day that they can't go to school and get an educa-

USING A WELL WE BUILT WITH
THE THIRST PROJECT

tion. "We visited a school full of kids struggling with these issues," Nash wrote on Twitter with a photo of him surrounded by kids. "Despite their struggles these kids were the most energetic, outgoing & genuinely happy kids I've ever met."

I felt true purpose doing that in Swaziland like never before. I am a full ambassador for the Thirst Project and will be for the rest of my life. But that's just scratching the surface. Every day I'm not doing something for the world I feel like I'm wasting my time.

Nash came home to L.A. from Africa with a very different perspective on the world.

I live completely differently after those two trips. I don't take anything for granted.

Stunned by the waste in America—of food, things, and, of course, water—Nash engages in a much more modest existence. He and Taylor live in a 1,200-square-foot house, where, as he puts it, "I have more than I could ever want." He no longer takes long showers or lets the faucets run. He remains a vegan. While he doesn't advocate that for everyone, Nash does want people to understand their impact on the environment.

Vegan or not you can still help the environment. Buy local, support small businesses and organic farming, swap plastic for reusable materials, cut out meat or dairy (or both) once a week. Every little thing we do has some sort of impact—it's beyond time to start acting like it.

Nash began growing food in his backyard, enlisting Hayes to move three hundred pounds of soil in one weekend to build a garden. Picking cherry tomatoes and peppers or weeding his zucchini plants, Nash has found much more enjoyment than he ever did at those crazy house parties he went to when he first arrived in L.A.

I had to stop being a consumer and become an observer to see that fulfillment is coming from doing what you want, how you want—not living for the hype.

Everything Nash does nowadays, he wants to have substance, which is the opposite of how he operated in the beginning. When he first started making Vines at Davidson Day, he utilized anything at his disposal to get as much attention from his classmates as he could. Although his audience grew bigger—much bigger—the premise didn't really change. The goal was to make a viral something. *Anything.*

It's a super-unhealthy way to live. I can tell you, as someone who has been posting for years for millions of people, there is no fulfillment from posting for the sole purpose of gaining attention and likes. That is so backward to growing as a person.

Jerome Jarre, the Vine star with whom Nash traveled to Iceland back at the start of his career, is a role model for him in the world of online influencers. Jerome once tweeted, "The best way to multiply your happiness is to share it with others." And he truly lives by those words. Although he's got a strong business head on his shoulders (he created one of the first agencies dedicated to Viners and Instagramers), he's also one of the leading activists in the world.

Jerome has done so much for so many causes, but he's also run his own career in a conscious way. He started the #uglyselfiechallenge in an effort to stem the growing preoccupation with taking the perfect picture of yourself. He put it out there on a Friday and by the end of the weekend there were more than 120,000 ugly selfies under his name or the hashtag he created for the movement.

But that pales in comparison to his Love Army. In 2017, Jerome came up with a "crazy idea" to fight famine in Somalia. The idea was to get Turkish Airlines, the only commercial airline that flew to Somalia, to donate a cargo plane for a huge food delivery. The campaign, which became known as "Love Army for Somalia," went viral. The actor Ben Stiller and the political activist and former quarterback Colin Kaepernick donated money and raised awareness for the effort. According to the American Refugee Committee, the Love Army "mobilized their 1 billion+ followers to send an outpouring of love and support to people struggling in Somalia. 95,000 people have joined the movement, and gifts as small as $5 added up to a staggering $2.7 million! As a result, we've been able to deliver 6 million liters of clean water and 1,300 tons of food to the hardest hit Somali families."

Wow. And that wasn't the end of the Love Army. Jerome mobilized the troops for Puerto Rico after the devastating Hurricane Maria—and then again in response to the refugee crisis of the Rohingyas. Most of this Muslim minority had to flee their homes in the predominately Buddhist country of Myanmar because of terrible persecution. In one year, the Love Army raised $2.2 million for the Rohingya people from 61,525 people all over the world.

Jerome has always put his ideals at the center of his work—even when it meant losing a lot of money. When one popular brand that he would only describe publicly as "an unhealthy food product" offered him $1 million to become a spokesman, Jerome declined. He didn't want to benefit financially by making other people's lives worse. This isn't typical for a guy whose Vines were viewed more than one billion times and caused crowds so big to come out to see him that riot police were called in.

He is so ahead of his time.

Another one of Nash's role models, although totally different from Jerome, is Bo Burnham, a multifaceted entertainer who got his start as a YouTuber back in 2006. The videos of him playing guitar or the electronic keyboard while singing original material he calls "pubescent musical comedy" went viral and led to him signing a record deal with Comedy Central Records. Although he had a lot of success with comedy, including two stand-up specials on Netflix, Bo continued to push himself creatively. He wrote a book of poetry, entitled *Egghead: Or, You Can't Survive on Ideas Alone.*

However it was Bo's first feature film, which he wrote and directed himself, that had the most emotional resonance for Nash—and many others. *Eighth Grade,* released in 2018, tells the story of thirteen-year-old Kayla, who has her own YouTube series, Kayla's Korner, where she makes videos with corny, awkward advice that are watched by . . . absolutely no one. Through the character of Kayla, actress Elsie Fisher perfectly portrays the combination of hope, desire, and painful shyness that hits home for most people who have lived through eighth grade. But as Owen Gleiberman, the chief film critic of *Variety,* wrote while calling Bo's film a "minor marvel," "The beauty of *Eighth Grade* is that it's highly specific and generational. It's the first movie to capture, in a major way, the teenage experience of those who have only existed on this planet during the digital era."

Ninety percent of stuff that gets made in the industry is for the hoopla. Bo Burnham's *Eighth Grade* is a huge inspiration for me. So is Jordan Peele's *Get Out.* Both those films are entertaining, but they also have meaning. They are saying things that matter.

Nash wants to find a balance between making culture that matters and then using that position to be an activist for disadvantaged communities and issues of importance.

I don't want to be Jackass 2.0.

He wants to be a person of substance, sharing things that matter, whether it's a piece of art or a shout-out, and not just come and go like a throwaway tweet. Nash admits to having been part of that wave of meaningless posts and regrets that millions of people paid attention and reacted to them. Now he posts a lot less, and fewer people might engage with what he puts out there. But he's okay with that.

FIRST TAKE

You need to fail in order to succeed. In fact, you often learn more from the bad than the good. There are lessons to be learned from every single thing.

It's easy to get blocked by negativity, boundaries, or unlucky circumstances. Nash has learned how to go forward in time in order to look backward. You can do the same thing.

It sounds strange, but it helps. Look past where you are now and transport yourself into the future, the one that you want for yourself. While you are there in your head, reflect back on your past. All this time travel will help you better understand your present and establish the connection that will take you where you want to be.

There's nothing that is 100 percent positive or 100 percent negative. Even if there is an ultimate good and ultimate bad hanging out somewhere in the universe, we live in the spectrum in between. Where you stand on that spectrum depends on how you live; your actions are the only determining factor. We create our own hell . . . and our own heaven.

And as I said to myself when I began my whole journey, if you can just change one person's life for the better, this whole thing will be worth it.

AFTERWORD

Hopefully at this point you feel at least a little inspired and motivated to make a difference, not only in the world but also in your life. You will not live a day in your life fully until you understand what it is that drives you crazy. You need to figure out who you really are and what your true purpose is. What is it that you can harness so that for the rest of your days, you aren't working to live but thriving and creating through your passion?

I implore all of you to please find that. I know each and every one of you can do it. But once you've done that, your work is not done. Once you've found your purpose, I need you to take advantage of it—and change the world with it. The greatest impact you can have on other people is by showing them how good you are at your craft; how you've perfected this, or done that.

I recognize that I'm one of the lucky ones on this earth. Not only was I born in the richest, most powerful country in the world, but I also came from a loving family where I was told my whole life, "You can do anything you set your mind to." Even with all the privilege, I still was confused. I can do whatever I set my mind to? What does that mean?

I didn't truly understand the meaning of my parents' words to me until I realized my purpose. Even though I had a lot of success at an early age, I'm still searching. But now I'm armed with the confidence that I can achieve whatever I want if I just put my mind to it and really focus. For example, I hope to return to school one day to study astronomy. That might sound like a stretch, but if I take the right courses and find the right teachers, I have nothing but the work in front of me, and that I know I can do.

I want everyone to experience this kind of confidence and freedom to dream.

Every kid goes to school and has his or her predetermined path in life, usually enforced by parents, beliefs, and social circumstances. But kids need to know that you can create your destiny. You can create your reality. Anything you can imagine can be real. Anything inside your head can be made in this world.

Many of us have iPhones, a powerful tool right in the palm of our hands to whip up any story we can dream up. The device has a 1080p camera, one of the best there is, and a mic of equal quality. So why isn't everyone making movies? Why isn't everyone telling stories? We have all the tools at our fingertips to not only spread our word to the masses, but to create what our word is—to figure out what's right, what's wrong, what's natural, what's not, what's good, what's bad. For our generation. The only thing keeping most of us back is our mind-set.

We don't need anything synthetic, anything produced, anything outside ourselves to change our thinking. All we need to do is open up ourselves in order to look both deep inside and far beyond ourselves. Change others' lives by changing your life.

I want to get this message out in a serious way. Just like different social media platforms have different calls to action, I felt that a book was the best way to deal with such a large, important, and imperative mission. Some stuff just doesn't fit on social media or in a video.

I believe that, at this point in reading this, you guys should all have the confidence and the ability to go out and create everything you want. Everything you can imagine can be real, and that's what I invite you all to do, because that's what it's all about.

NASH FACTS

- I was dead silent when I came out of the womb. My mom was worried something was wrong with me, because my brother Will was born with the umbilical cord wrapped around his neck. But I was just looking around the room.

- I'm a vegan.

- I make the best nachos.

- Yellow mustard is the life.

- I break a phone or a bone every month.

- I have watched every episode of *Friends* at least eight times. (I did the same thing with *Freaks and Geeks*.)

- I don't believe in flowers as decoration, because as soon as you pick a flower it's dead.

- I like one-of-a-kind everything.

- I never wear deodorant.

- The first movie I ever watched was *Titanic* (I was like a week old and my mom was really the one watching it).